Cancer? But I'm a Virgo.
(This is not a book about astrology.*)
*It is a book about cancer.

WRITTEN BY
JOHNNY BROOKBANK

Jade, thank you so much for standing by me through the most difficult time of my life.
You are amazing and brave and kind and incredible and I can never pay you back.

I can never pay you back. And I hope that the opportunity to do so never arises.

Thank you for supporting me through this entire insane book. Thank you for continuing to support my wild ideas, dreams, and goals over the last 15 years. We have gone to the ends of the earth together and I could not have done any of this alone.

Your spirit is beautiful.

Thank you for standing next to me.

-Johnny

Mom, how do I say thank you for sacrificing your personal life and living with us and bringing me back from the dead? How do I thank you for the first gift that you gave me? My life. Without it, none of this, good or bad, would be possible. And I will take all of the bad in order to experience the good every single time. Thank you for giving me the chance to thrive in this weird and wonderful world and thank you for always encouraging me to be strange.

You are amazing and selfless and irreplaceable.
You have given me life and then you helped me preserve it.

To say I owe you one would be an understatement.

But I do. I owe you a couple for sure.

-Charlie Brown

PROLOGUE

It's my twenty-sixth birthday and I'm standing in front of a rotund Indian man with my pants around my ankles, my wiener hanging limply between us like a sad-faced emoticon. He gently pats the paper-covered exam table with his meaty hand and in his thick accent says, "Please sit up here."

I pull myself onto the table, no easy feat with my pants bunched on top of my sneakers and my hands cupped neatly around my genitals for the sake of modesty. The ultrasound technician takes a seat on a low stool next to me, pinches my noodle between his thumb and forefinger and says, "Hold this, but don't pull on it." First, this is everything nightmares are made of. Second, I can't help but stop to wonder what kinds of patients typically find themselves in this room. Men who, when confronted with a white-robed stranger, posters of bisected colons, and the aroma of cleaning supplies, are suddenly thrown into such an erotic frenzy that they simply must begin to "pull on it."

I lie back and hear the sound of two rubber gloves being stretched and adjusted over as many large hands, the latex squeaking against itself. The noise sends a shiver up my spine, and the sterile smell in the air turns my stomach.

I just want this over. I just want an answer.

The Indian Man says, "I'm going to apply the jelly now," and I'm thankful for the heads up because, lying here today, I have no idea what to expect anymore. Things have been spiraling quickly out of control for about a month. There are too many questions cropping up without near enough answers. My life has become a really terrible episode of *LOST*, except there are no polar bears or time travel or bad CG smoke monsters . . . .

He begins to gently rub the cold gel on my nut sack when, making a desperate stab at comedy, I nervously blurt out, "Hey, man, you've got the best seat in the house!" I say it as a joke. I say it to lighten the mood. I say it because I'm afraid I'm going to die, and I need to laugh.

The Indian Man completely disregards my comment and instead pulls out an ultrasound gun that he places against the taut skin of my scrotum (the room feels like a brisk 64 degrees and my body is adjusting accordingly). As he snaps several high-contrast black and white photos of my testicle, I shut my eyes and pretend that I am somewhere else; in the parking lot, at work, at home, in outer space. I attempt to force myself to have an out-of-body experience. I want to step away and come back when this is all over and hopefully "all over" is in just a few moments and not several months or years from now.

I open my eyes and see, on the ceiling directly above me, a little sign that reads, I'D RATHER BE FISHING. I begin to count the dots in the tiles, one hundred, one thousand, one million little pinholes above me, and I place my mind inside each one. The Indian Man takes his time and is very thorough in, what is for him, a routine scanning procedure. For me it is everything.

The silence is palpable. I can feel it in every pore of my body. I can sense the electric buzz from the machine where, as I glance over, I can actually *see* my testicle for the first time in my life. It just rests there like an enormous black and white egg filled with hope and desperation and anxiety and sperm. The quiet resting too heavy on my shoulders, I break it with, "Is it a boy or a girl?"

The Indian Man doesn't smile at the joke. Instead, he simply states, "It's a tumor."

PART 1

"Insert pithy yet poignant quote here that signifies the beginning of a long but life-changing journey."

CHAPTER 1
THE DESERT

It's 5:45 a.m., and the sky is just beginning to lighten, turning from black, to shades of gray, to purple, to orange, same as a bruise. The sun just begins to peek over the mountains directly in front of me, and it's one of the most beautiful and serene things I've ever seen.

I stare directly into the glowing orb and watch it rise, rise, rise, until it's a blazing white-hot inferno too bright to look at. I roll my window down and the warm desert wind hits me in the face. After driving straight through a chilly night, it's the perfect temperature. I crank the stereo; Zack de la Rocha's latest band, *One Day as a Lion,* has just released its first five-track EP, and it has been my soundtrack from Los Angeles to Las Vegas for the past several hours.

The wind blows in my ears so I turn the music up louder. I turn the music up louder. I turn the music up louder. It's at maximum volume and I am simply screaming alongside the lyrics, shaking my head and pounding the steering wheel. Whenever a car approaches, I quickly compose myself, pretending to just be a regular guy driving a regular family-friendly car on a regular freeway. As soon as I'm sure the car is out of sight, I resume my full-body-dry-heave inspired dance moves. Remember, dance like no one is watching . . . unless someone actually is. I am Axl Rose. I am Anthony Kiedis. I am Andrew W.K.

I slowly push my foot toward the floor and watch as the speedometer begins its sluggish ascent up the numeric Mount Everest built into my dashboard—75 . . . 80 . . . 90 mph . . . . I lock it in and cruise, watching cactus and dirt blur past me on the left and right. There is a certain freedom in the desert, a dirty voice that calls out to let everything go . . . a voice that is Reckless Abandon.

At this time of morning, there are almost no cars on the highway so, like a horny high school boy, I begin to nudge a little further, just to see what'll happen: 95 . . . 96 . . . 97 . . . 98 . . . . I've never pushed this or any other car to 100 mph, and being this close makes me want to just stick it in and slam it down.

I take a deep breath, hold it, and juice the pedal. The gage immediately leaps like someone has jammed a cattle prod into the base of its skull . . . 99 . . . 100 . . . 105 . . . 110 . . . 115. At 120 mph I scream out the window at the top of my lungs.

I am twenty-five. It's one month before my birthday, and I am invincible.

Nothing can touch me.

Nothing.

CHAPTER 2
THE ORANGE AND THE SOCK

I am six years old, and I know that something is wrong with me. It's something that stretches far beyond the reaches of the faux-fashionable brown mullet that frames my over-sized head, making me look like the Son of Frankenstein. The wrongness is not the cold sore on my mouth that has been emblazoned into so many family photos from that year. It is not my excessively bushy eyebrows that look like storm clouds.

The year is 1988, and the *wrongness* has always been. It isn't something that came about or was discovered one day. It is something that I've simply grown horribly accustomed to, the way someone who lives next door to an airport may eventually drown out the jet engines with their own thoughts.

I have only one testicle.

Or rather, I have two. But the second is undescended, just chilling out in my six-year-old abdomen, afraid to come down into its hormone hammock. I know this is unnatural and wrong and I've thought about it every single day for as long as I've understood its *wrongness*. For as long as I've understood that boys have *two* and I have *one*, I have dwelt on its absence. For as long as I can remember, this has been my body.

One day, after spending an inordinate amount of time contemplating my testicle, I decide to approach my mother about the issue.

I go upstairs to their bedroom where my mother is folding laundry. The question burns in my stomach and in my throat, and I don't want to say it because, even though she is my mother . . . *she is my mother* . . . and I don't want to talk to her about my privates.

"Mom?" I begin. She sets aside one of my dad's brown military shirts, folds her hands in her lap and smiles with a welcoming air. This is her finest quality; she will give you everything she has, every ounce of attention, every piece of love she can muster. It belongs to you.

I lean in the doorway and fidget awkwardly. I look down at my sneakers. I look down at my zipper, guarding my dirty secret like a monster with a hundred teeth.

"Why . . . do I only . . . have one . . .?" and I can't even bring myself to say that final word, afraid it will just hang awkwardly between us like a vampire.

"One what, honey?"

Today, there are hundreds of synonyms for it. Then, I knew only one and the word choked me. I stare down at the brown almost-shag-but-not-quite carpeting, dirty with white dog hair. I look up and begin fiddling mindlessly with the doorjamb, reaching out and running my finger over the wooden plank. I expel my breath and quickly cough the syllable out as nonchalantly as possible.

"Ball."

My hands convulsively go toward my crotch, and I feel dirty and perverse having said the word in front of my *mother*. We often forget as adults that children know shame, true and terrible shame that dwarfs our own. Children lack the proper familiarity that they are not alone in their experiences. To them, the world is happening for the first time, and the world only exists in the bubble of their own realities.

As a man, you can accept who you are, and you can own it. Your flaws can become quirks that you wear proudly, if not a bit oddly. As a child, you are simply different from everyone else, and at six years old, I am extremely ashamed about my secret, and I want nothing more than to be Normal.

My mother tells me that my "ball" is up in my tummy and that it's been that way since I was born. She tells me that the doctor says it will just come down one day, *abracadabra*. It's simply going to appear again like a mysterious second uncle.

She tells me that, after the doctor found it, he never checked again, never followed up—that during all my infant appointments, it was never rectified. As a man, when I press her and ask, "Why didn't *you* do something? Say something?" She says, "I eventually stopped changing your diapers and then . . . " She shrugs sadly as the thought trails off.

As a boy, I cry about it often and the tears add to my shame and eat away at me from the inside like a cancer. Eventually, after not just *months* of living like this but *years*, I finally bring the issue back to my mother's attention.

"*When? When* is my *bawl* coming back down?" and I say it just like that, *bawl* instead of *ball*. I really lay the emphasis on the inflection, spitting out the word like venom. I am eight years old now and I've never felt so much as a rumble from the mythical Loch Nut Monster.

Sometimes I try pushing on my abdomen, hoping to cause a miraculous healing. I imagine an "extra" testicle just suddenly slopping down and filling up my nut sack like an orange in an old sock and *voila* problem solved.

This does not happen.

As the year progresses, larger questions begin surfacing in my mind. The Big Questions. The Long-Distance Questions that perhaps no normal third grader has any reason to be thinking. But I am no Normal third grader. I am a child who spends endless hours meditating on his genitals and pressing on his abdomen, hoping to give birth to a testicle.

What happens when I get married? The thought drops in my lap like a cinder block. I'm going to have to tell a *girl* about my secret. This prospect is worse than anything I have ever imagined. I try to conjure up the conversation in my head. Would I tell her before we were wed? Would I tell her after we were married? Would I tell her on our wedding day so that we've already spent a bunch of money and our families were all there and she wouldn't be able to run away? Yes, that's the way I'll do it. I'll trap her!

First comes love, then comes marriage, then comes the . . . . A heaviness fills me, and something I had never considered strikes me like a slap on the face. *Fertility. Potency. Mobility.* These are not words that I understand, but they are words whose meanings I comprehend. Can a man create babies if he is lacking half of his equipment? I'm imagining a jet with one wing. I'm imagining a gun with no bullets. I'm imagining a dick with no *bawls*.

At a third-grade level, I fully understand the basic concept of where babies come from—insert Tab A into Slot B. But I don't understand what happens when one of the key components has gone AWOL. I don't understand the science behind it. Is one a positive charge and one a negative charge? Do you need them both to create some kind of high-powered, special juice? Is one the fluid and one the sperm?

My life is crumbling before it's even begun, and my mental state is collapsing. I rush home after school and begin demanding action from my mother.

"Where is my *bawl?! I want it back! It's mine! I want to see a doctor, and I want him to fix me*."

***   ***   ***   ***   ***

This is the first time I've had any kind of physical done. I'd never been in any type of sport, so I'd never been required to go through the customary "Turn your head and cough" routine. I am terribly nervous as I sit in the waiting room, my hands sweating, my foot bouncing. This is the first time that anyone outside of my mother will know my secret, and this person will discover it by *touching* me. I am eight, and I am about to be fully exposed in front of a stranger in the most intimate fashion possible. As I wait, instead of reading a magazine, I just stare at a Georgia O'Keeffe painting, an artist whose work I will become well acquainted with in roughly twenty years.

"Johnny . . . Broogbank?" People more often than not say my last name with a question mark and a randomly misplaced letter. My mother and I stand up, and in the back hall they measure me, weigh me, blood pressurize me, and escort me into a broom closet adorned with more Georgia O'Keeffe specials.

I stand up and begin to pace wildly while cracking my knuckles. My mother suggests that I relax because the doctor has "seen it all" and I care little and less because I have seen "almost nothing" and I've never had a grown man fondle my package before and I find the idea to be terribly off-putting, even at eight. Or rather, *especially* at eight.

14

There is a gentle knock at the door, and I immediately know that we have entered The Point of No Return. My stomach drops and all the butterflies inside of it take flight. He enters the room, a stethoscope around his neck, and his physical features immediately remind me of the pink Franken Berry cartoon character on the cereal box, enormous and hulking, thick in the shoulders, hairy hands, but a kind face with a gentle smile.

Dr. Franken Berry asks my mother and me a few questions in that friendly but sterile tone that most GPs have before tapping the table and telling me to "Pull down my pants and hop up here." I fumble slowly with my belt and then, in sheer neurosis, I ask, "Underwear too?" and he replies in the affirmative.

And it's in that next moment while bent in half, my hands clutching the waistband on my very tight, very white undies that I wonder why I asked my mother to come here with me.

Dr. Franken Berry feels around my abdomen and begins pressing and I almost tell him, "Don't bother, I've been trying that technique for years," but instead say nothing. He grabs my *bawl* and says, "Turn your head to the left . . . and cough. Turn your head to the right . . . " and I see my mom sitting in the chair. She looks so sad. Her eyes are downcast and she fiddles with her fingernails. I am glad she's here, and I am glad she's looking away, supporting me quietly in my shame. " . . . And cough."

He tells us we need to do surgery to try and draw it down and I am joyous, celebratory even. I am going to be *whole*. I am going to have *two* testicles. Two *bawls*. Like an x-rated version of Pinocchio, I'm going to be a real boy.

I'm pulled out of school for the operation because I will be hospitalized for three days, the entirety of which are all very blurry to me. The tent-pole moments I will highlight are as follow.

I am all alone on a gurney in a hallway. A male nurse approaches me and says he's going to give me an IV. I've never had one, and I am horrified. I see the size of the needle and my horror turns to terror. He rubs my arm and massages it and slaps it and then says, "All done." The man was an artist and his craft so perfect and painless that, to this day, it is the IV that I rate all others by.

Inside the operating room, I count backward from ten and only get to nine before I black out from the anesthetic.

My next memory is laughing with my mom in the recovery room. Some commercial has come on that consists of a talking roll of toilet paper, and I believe I am able to recall this specific moment so vividly not because of the humor but because of the pain, which is intense and, very literally, sidesplitting. The surgeon has cut a three-and-a-half-inch gash on the right side of my groin, and I can hear it scream every time my muscles cinch up. What he did in there, I have no idea, but it feels like I've been stuffed full of hot thumbtacks. Laughing and crying, I ask my mom to turn off the television and to please stop imitating the talking toilet paper.

My next and final memory of the hospital is me asking my mom, "Did they do it?" and her simply saying, "No," and I am so crushed that I weep in my bed. I am eight years old and the finality of it is the worst news I've ever had in my life. I will forever have only one testicle. One *bawl*. I don't want to talk. I don't want to listen. I just want to forget.

Perhaps this seems overdramatic, but to a young boy, fitting in is the world, and I've just been told that I will forever be different and not simply through the color of my hair or my height or my language but by the one thing that makes a boy a boy.

A doctor enters the room to check my incision. It is the first time I've seen my wound and the sight disgusts me. My skin on either side of the cut has been pinched together and folded over itself and then sutured through a number of times. It looks like someone has laid a thick string of flesh-colored, chewed up bubblegum across my skin and then threaded it with long spider legs. The smell is foul. It is yellow and blue and dripping fluids but the doctor says it looks fine, which I take as an extremely relative deduction.

He asks me if I have any questions and I do. It's one that I have to know the answer to but am horrified to ask for fear of the truth, for fear of more bad news. I simply say, "Can I still have kids?"

The doctor looks at me and just chuckles and says, "Yeah. You can still have kids. Think of your second testicle like a spare tire. It's just in case."

Just in case, I think. Yeah. After all, what are the chances I'd lose my backup, as well?

The doctor leaves and my mother, at a failed attempt to make me feel better says something poetic like, "It was all shriveled up and dead so they had to pull it out. They said if we'd left it in there for another week it could have caused cancer."

It is a phrase that I will revisit frequently in my life, wondering if something was left behind, lying dormant, waiting . . . .

CHAPTER 3
PLAGUED BY PLAGUES

Eczema. Ring worms. Food poisoning. Poison poisoning. West Nile. Airborne toxins. Flu, cold, constipation, diarrhea. I have suffered from it all, both real and imaginary. My wife points an accusing finger at me and says, *"You're a hypochondriac!"* and I casually walk into the other room, get online, and look up the disease to see if I am actually exhibiting symptoms.

Illnesses are my passion and I collect them like stickers in a book. In elementary school, I had ulcers. In junior high, insomnia. In high school, I became convinced that I had acquired early onset Alzheimer's because I couldn't remember any of the mathematical equations that help you solve endless rows of meaningless problems. It seemed to come so easily to everyone else. . . .

Years later, a friend will tell me that his son can't seem to get a grasp on numeric sequences. More than just a few in a row and *"Poof,"* he says, "they're gone." He tells me the disease is called *dyscalculia* and it simply sounds too similar to *Dracula* for me to pass up. I'm positive I have it. I wear it on my sleeve, displaying the fact proudly. I won't let my handicap hold me back. I won't box it up in some closet. Plus, I've always been a bit more of a words guy and less of a digits person anyway so I feel like there is something strangely poetic in my illness, my disease, my burden.

My wife says, "You don't have dyscalculia. You're just an idiot." I look up the term *idiot* on Web MD betting that she's right but no results return. Further research is required.

*** *** *** *** ***

My stomach rolls over, and I vomit into a toilet, beads of sweat dripping down my forehead. My knees are raw from kneeling on the bathroom tiles. My wife circles the door frame, blocking the light shining dramatically on my face and says, uncaringly, "You're going to be late for work."

"I can't go to work! Look at me! I'm sick!" I plead, desperately trying to make her understand. It's not cancer, not yet (this is still years and years earlier), but it's definitely something.

"You're not sick." I puke again just to reinforce my point and then elaborately throw myself onto the bathroom floor, the back of my hand pressed against my sort-of-hot forehead. Not sick? *Not sick?* Has she *heard* of the norovirus?! Because I have it on good account (my friend's friend is pre-med) that it's making rounds this year. A couple people died in Missouri. Didn't my wife hear about this? Doesn't she watch the news on Comedy Central? Doesn't she read *The Onion*?

She tells me that I don't have the norovirus. She tells me that I have the moron virus and then she laughs at her own dumb little joke while I just dry heave twice in a row. I tell her to look away. I tell her that the norovirus is really taking its toll on me when suddenly my chest is racked with a pinching suffocation. It feels like someone is pulling the membrane off my lungs every time I inhale. Jade raises an eyebrow and says, "*Pleurisy* again?"

I just hold up a hand for her to "be silent" while I bare my cross. She says, "Oh, geeeeez." After the pain passes I explain that, "I have pleurisy," and she says, "I know you think you do," and I say, "It's an inflammation of the lining on the lungs," and she says, "You've told me the definition," and I say, "My mom has it too," and my wife says, "I'm sure she believes she does."

Is there nothing I can do to convince her of my various conditions? Is it my fault I have an immune system that is susceptible to such attacks? *Someday*, I tell myself, *someday I'll get something and she'll believe me.*

Jade says, "Are you day dreaming about your illnesses?" and I say, "Huh? What?" and she says, "Wishing someone would believe that your fake thing was real?" and I say, "My fake thing *is* real. Remember The Blood Shit Incident?"

Jade says, "*I* remember The Blood Shit Incident. I wonder if *you* remember it." I say, "Of *course* I remember it. I was there. I *wrote* it." And she says, "Every piece of good fiction needs an author."

*** *** *** *** ***

I'm sitting on the toilet in my mom's house and I'm staring at a piece of toilet paper covered in brown and red. I'm shitting blood. It's been happening for a couple days. Not a lot. Just a little. Just a few drops. Just enough to fill a vile. Or two.

I'm nineteen and I try to weigh my options—the possibilities, the probabilities, the causes, the outcomes. "Why would my ass be bleeding?" I ask myself. "I don't stick things up it. I swear."

Who do I approach? Who do I ask for advice? Not my dad. Definitely not my mother; I don't want to see the sequel to The Nut Sack Situation. No, I'll handle this one myself. How to proceed, how to proceed. The Internet? Too traceable. The search engines all have a way of remembering things I type in, and I'm no good with PCs. I don't understand how to clear the cash or eat the cookies or whatever. The library? Absolutely not. The idea of checking out a book about anal fissures will certainly get me on some Pervert of the Week list.

Finally, after meditating on the rhythmic *drip-drip-drip*, the answer comes to me clearly, like a comet in the night sky. It is a moment of what some may call divine clarity. It is so simple I can't believe I didn't see it before.

I will simply ignore the problem and hope it fixes itself.

I am a *human body*! I get scratches and cuts all the time and what happens? Blood clotting, scabbing . . . something . . . something else, science, etc., and there you have it, back to normal! My inner ass cavern will be the same! I just need to leave it be and give it some time to heal. I'll eat soft foods. I'll push very, *very* gently. Or maybe not at all. I'll practice Zen meditation and just let the fecal matter slither from my rectum like a snake shedding skin.

This could work. This could definitely work.

Two weeks later, I'm still shitting blood. It's not slowing down. *What was I thinking?!* Scabs?! Inside my ass?! What if there are ruptures and the blood ruptures are being infected by feces? Don't people *die* when their shit and blood begin to mix?

My stomach hurts. My head hurts. *IT'S HAPPENING!*

Could I bring this to my girlfriend? Could I ask Jade about this? *Yeah!* She's *really* smart. A grade-A student through and through, she was studying to become a neonatologist and you *know* anyone with the suffix *-ologist* in their job title is legit.

She knows things I don't know. She understands things about blood and bile and positrons and neutrons and Klingons and she pretty much just knows everything! She'll know . . . she'll know. But how do I breach the topic? This is touchy stuff, and it's important not to make it weird. Then the answer comes to me clearly, like a comet in the night sky. It is a moment of what some may call divine clarity. It is so simple I can't believe I didn't see it before. The words come to me with such smooth precision it is as though a greater entity is speaking directly through me.

We're sitting at the table, alone, at my house, eating jam-covered waffles. She smiles at me and I say, "I've been shitting blood for three weeks now. What do you suppose this—" she drops her fork, but I finish my thought anyway, "—could mean?"

Coming from a world where it took eight years to get my missing testicle examined by a doctor, I was made strangely uncomfortable by the speed at which Jade scheduled an appointment for me later that same day. Neither of us knew it then, me nineteen, she just turning eighteen, but we were being given a small glimpse into our future, more than a decade away: The Caretaker and The Ass Bleeder.

I love her. I am nineteen and I know this. I love her for all of the fantastic things she is, says, and does, but I love her because I can tell her that I'm shitting blood and she is willing to get her hands (figuratively) dirty to solve it. She's had commitment from day one. She's a barnacle. She's not letting go.

The next day, sitting again in the stagnant, falsely fresh smelling waiting room of my local clinic, I find myself staring at those same Georgia O'Keeffe paintings and wondering, "Where do they come from? Who is Georgia O'Keeffe? Why do all hospitals and clinics insist on using her work?"

I lean over to Jade and I ask (since she knows everything), "What do you think they'll do? Do you think I'll just get some pills or cream?" and Jade answers, "He's probably going to take a speculum—" and I cut her off.

"Sorry. A what?"

"A speculum."

"What's a speculum?"

"Oh, it's like this thing they put in your vagina and they turn this crank and it opens you up so they can get a really good view. They'll probably do that to your ass."

My face goes white. My blood turns to ice. She knows *everything*.

I say to her, "They've done this to you?" and she says, "Yeah. Couple times," and I say, "And you think they're going to—are you messing with me?" and she says, "No. They're checking to see if you have blood fissures. They need to look. So they need to *spread*."

25

I stand up. I am *done*. I will go with Plan B: The Scabbing Over Plan. But Jade grabs my hand before I can run and tells me to sit down. I think she's going to say she's just joking but instead she says, "Bleeding from your butt can mean colon cancer and men eighteen and up need to be getting checked regularly."[*]

---

[*]Fact. So if you find the dirty death star dripping darkness, dash to the doc and have your derriere dissected.

I say, "But the speculum . . . ?" and she finishes with, "Oh yeah, they're shoving that thing way up there and parting you like the Red Sea."

I stand up and begin heading toward the door when the nurse calls me, "Johnny . . . Buh . . . rookbag?" Every eye in the room lands on me, the guy standing up, looking like a deer in headlights. The nurse speaks softly, over the shuffle of papers and various weekly literature, "Right this way."

Before disappearing into the halls, I turn back and take one last look at Jade who is sitting in her chair, a gossip magazine on her lap, spreading her hands open, miming a speculum.

I hate her.

But not the kind of hate that means I'm going to burn her house down. I mean the kind where you know they know better and they're making you do something that's necessary even though you don't want to.

Inside the doctor's office there is no cancer, there are no fissures or ruptures and there is, thankfully, no speculum. There is only a man with a rubber glove, a bunch of lube and a strange eagerness to examine me. In the end he gives me some pills and some cream and says to eat soft foods and to not press so hard. He tells me that the human body is an amazing thing and that I'll be just fine.

It'll heal itself.

I shrug and shake my head and walk back to the lobby, where I eyebrow beat Jade to death. We hold hands and walk out into the sunlight while Fate sits back on its haunches and laughs, waiting eagerly for us to return on this path sooner rather than later. It watches our backs as we fade from sight, the glossy luster of blissful ignorance protecting us like armor.

We are still young, only nineteen. And neither of us have ever been struck with the harsh reality of true tragedy. We just don't know anything yet.

But we very soon will.

CHAPTER 4
FIRST CONTACT

I pull into my driveway around 11:30 p.m. I've spent the last two days in Vegas smoking enough pot to transform my brain into one of those slimy slug-souls from *The Little Mermaid.* The house is mostly dark save for a small desk lamp radiating a warm glow in the front window. Like the jingle of that popular hotel, my wife has left a light on for me. The trip back from Las Vegas was mostly uneventful (outside of me having to shit off my front bumper but that story is neither here nor there); the trip driving west always lacks any of the magic of the possibility that crackles in the air when heading toward the Electric City. I haven't slept more than a few scattered hours in two days and I can feel it.

When I finally open my front door, I immediately feel the warm welcome that is Home. My wife has an aura about her that allows her to take the mundane and turn it into the extraordinary. Our house is no longer wood and dry wall. It is flesh and bone and personality. It is living and breathing and welcoming. She chooses color palettes and purchases knick knacks; the bar-style dining-room table, the weird collection of antique cameras on top of the shelves in the kitchen, the vintage teacher's desk in the living room, the furniture, the mirrors, the finds, the little treasures. I try to imagine what I would have done to this house if I'd lived here alone, if we'd never gotten married.

I'm seeing white walls. I'm seeing a stained couch. I'm seeing pizza boxes. Maybe I'm a little heavier? Maybe I sleep on a pile of wood chips in the corner? An old blanket tangled around my ankle?

I sit down on my couch and I close my eyes, letting images of the weekend roll through my imagination: Caesar's Palace, The Venetian, the games, the walking, the laughing, the people, the servers dressed like Alice Cooper and Michael Jackson and Madonna. I chuckle to myself, having proudly taken that right of passage into Manhood that is Las Vegas. I'm 26 and at the top of the world.

Finally settled in, I pull out my pipe and stash of weed. The smoke fills my lungs and I quickly begin to disconnect from the world. So I lost $400? So what?! What's money? It's just paper. It's just representative of something. Take my money, take my job. I'd rather move into the woods, anyway. Lose myself in the trees, get out of the city. I hate the city—the smog, the traffic, the cement. I want clear blue skies and trees and rivers and rocks and animals and stars.

I have to pee.

I stand up and walk to the bathroom, down the dark hallway, bumping into the doorframe. I flip on a light and there, sitting in the corner, is the toilet. It's all come to this. My whole life has come to this toilet. Every step I've ever taken has led me right here. The first part of The Journey that is my life is about to end. Every choice, every waking moment has brought me here, to this bathroom, in this house, in this room, at this time, in this mental condition.

I reach down and fumble with my zipper, pulling it south. I reach inside my jeans and think briefly about my one testicle—its existence a constant reminder of the missing twin—and I start to pee. I stare at the red wall in front of me, thinking, *Bright red paint. That's a bold choice for my wife to go with. But she did it. I wonder what people think when they're standing here fondling their nut sacks and peeing?*

I look down and realize that I am, indeed, fondling my nut sack. This is a simple truth of the world; men just sometimes absent-mindedly grab handfuls of themselves and we bumble around blindly. It's like a security blanket. It's platonic. It's like petting a dog.

Mid-pee, mid-stream, mid-relief, my left hand feels something that does not belong. A foreign object on my body, a second tongue, a third nipple, a fourth knuckle—it's not right, not normal, not standard. It's the size of a pea and rests casually on my single remaining testicle.

And this is *the moment* where my life breaks in two. I don't know it yet but this is the moment of impact. Nothing will ever be as it was. Nothing will ever be the same.

Imagine with me . . . try to set aside all of your individual predispositions and personality traits. Listen to the stories I've told you about myself, pick up my luggage, my emotional baggage, my history of illness (both real and imagined) and touch my genitals with me. Imitate me. Channel me. Possess me. Feel the lump on your singular ball.

Also, you are pretty high right now.

I turn the pea over and over in my hand like a pebble, examining it, touching it, feeling it, becoming familiar with it. No. I can't become familiar with it. I know that immediately. We will never be friends. The hypochondriac begins whispering in my ear. He knows what it is. He, the great soothsayer of sickness knows what is happening right now. Whatever it is (you know what it is) I know that I hate it. Whatever it is (you know, just say it), I'm sure it will all go away soon. Just avert your eyes and breathe and (CANCER!) it will all be over soon.

Cancer . . . .

A woman tells me that she's pregnant. She tells me that it's crazy and exciting and wonderful. She tells me that she knew she was pregnant before the test results. She tells me that she *just knew* . . . and right now . . . I need no more explanation than that. I understand completely.

Cancer . . . .

I zip it back into my pants and stare at the red wall and think, " . . . . " and then I walk out of the bathroom, down the long hallway, and into my bedroom, where my wife is asleep. I wonder how she'll take the news. Will she cry? Weep? Fall into a great depression? Will we cling to one another for mutual comfort, swearing fealty to each other? Swearing that we'll get through this, don't worry, no matter what, etc., etc., etc.? I try to summon images of Hollywood movies into my mind; how have I seen this done? How did Mandy Moore break the news in *A Walk to Remember*?

Jade opens her eyes and says, "You're back. How was Vegas?" and I say, "Good," and I say, "There's something on my . . . . " and it's weird but I am six years old again, and I'm talking to my mom about my *bawl*, and I don't want to say it.

"What time is it?" she asks in a gravelly voice. "Late," I answer tenderly, quietly, wanting to keep things as calm as possible for the storm that is about to erupt. "It's around midnight." She asks me if I'm coming to bed.

I sit down and run my hands through her hair, the words in my throat, on my tongue, my lips. I say, "I felt something on my testicle. It's a lump. I think . . . I think I have . . . cancer."

There is a pause. She looks at me and blinks, once, twice, and I know some great emotion is on the precipice of bursting inside of her. She shuts her eyes, takes a breath and says, "You are such a hypochondriac. You have *cancer* now? Please." And she clicks off the bed lamp, leaving me in the literal, figurative, and metaphysical dark.

I am furious (scared). I am angry (confused). I am full of questions, and I want (need) answers. An idea hits me, and I do that thing that no one should ever, ever, *ever* do when they think they have cancer growing on their nuts and are super *super* high at the same time.

I get on the Internet and do a Google search for "Hard balls on balls" and the first option is a gay pornographic website starring body builders. I try again. "Infected nuts," and this time it's something about oak trees being poisoned. I try again, "How to check for testicular cancer" and the first hit says, "How to check for testicular cancer." Bingo.

Article after article after article pops up, an encyclopedia of penial knowledge at my shaft tip all for me to soak in and fear by myself in this paranoid state. "This most certainly will be a night I will never forget," I think to myself as one hand scrolls the text around the monitor and the other pinches that little peapod on my privates.

The first article says, "Take a warm bath, loosen up, pinch your nuts like this. Does the tumor feel like a little rock? Is it the size of a pea? Does it lack feeling? Then it's probably cancer."

Red flag, red flag, red flag. Cancer, cancer, cancer. Tumor, tumor, tumor. That's the first time I'd seen that word as it related to me. I was looking at the word *tumor*, and I was touching something *in my body* that may or may not have been (I know it is) a *tumor a tumor a cancerous tumor inside of my body I have cancer tumors cancer tumors cancer tumors.*

Maybe it's just a fluke, this article. Maybe I'm seeing what I want to see, believing what I want to believe, y'know? I *want* to know that what Jade is saying is correct. I'm a hypochondriac, and none of it is real. I click on another article but it says the same thing. Article three and four are likewise. By article eleven, my hope is not simply beginning to break, it is broken.

I. Just. Know.

PART 2

"What is to give light, must endure
burning."
-Viktor E. Frankl . . . whoever he is

CHAPTER 5
BIRTHDAY PRESENT

I'm sitting in a waiting room somewhere in Pasadena, staring at a magazine that is listing the 100 most influential people of the year. Lady Gaga, Jay-Z, and Bill Gates are all in attendance. I do a quick scan but don't see any glossy celebrity snapshots of Jesus.

The waiting room is empty. The couch I'm sitting on is leather and cold. I touch it with my finger and wonder if the cow that this skin belonged to had a nice personality. I touch my tumor by squeezing it between my thighs. It's still there. Maybe this doctor will simply give me some pills, and I can wipe all the sweat off my brow.

The woman behind the bulletproof glass calls my name, and I walk through a locked door. They weigh me, measure me, etc., etc. The nurse leaves, and I'm sitting alone in the Examination Room. The walls are covered in pictures that children have drawn in crayons, all with personalized messages addressed to a man named Dr. Odegaard.

"Thanks for fixing my arm," wrote James, 7, with a drawing of himself in a cast, standing in front of a tree. The drawing is so bad I have to wonder if he had to create it with his lesser-used hand.

"You're the best. Thank you for the Band-Aids," wrote Tiffany, 6, who decided to draw birds flying over a rainbow.

I try to imagine what my drawing would look like. There would be a picture of a smiling rooster. Above it, in bubble typeface, it would read, "Thanks for saving my dick. I owe you one." –Johnny, 26.

The doctor enters and asks me a few questions. First the preliminary stuff because it's my first visit to see him, followed by the more intimate inquiries. "What seems to be the problem?" And, "Describe the lump." And, "Which testicle is it on?" And this is where I sort of mumble something about a trick question. Mumble something about my uni-testicle. Mumble some off-colored joke that he doesn't laugh at. He asks me to pull my pants down, and I ask him if the door is locked. He tells me that no one will come in, and I comply.

He snaps on a rubber glove and fondles me in a professional manner. He hums and grunts a couple times, makes the sort of noise you might make after seeing a two-headed turtle—not absolute shock but more of an idle fascination.

He tells me to pull my pants up and that he definitely feels something. He tells me that he's recommending me to a good friend of his, a urologist (*penis doctor*; see also *dick doc*) named Dr. Honda. It's the 11th of September, and it will be six more

40

days with this thing growing inside of me before I get any real answers.

*** *** *** *** ***

On September 17, 2008, I turned 26 years old. My wife and I spent it indoors, she having made me a cake and purchased me a few books. The day was regular enough, the cake was regular enough, the weather was regular enough and, as far as birthdays go, it would forever be branded in my brain as the most irregular day I had ever experienced.

We arrive at Dr. Honda's office, a nice brick building in Arcadia, just after noon. My wife and I sit down in the lobby and she immediately picks up a *Better Homes* magazine and begins scouring it for ideas to, presumably, make our home . . . better.

Everyone in the room with us is old. Really old. Nursing-home old. They're so old, that they each have some kind of caretaker visiting the facility with them. I try to imagine the day, hundreds and hundreds of years from now, when I'll be too weak to take care of myself. The day, thousands of years from now when I can't bathe myself any longer. The day when I eat more pills than food. Millions of years away.

My wife turns to me and says, "What do you think he's going to say?" and I say, "You *know* what I think," and she just laughs and shrugs. She still thinks it's a cyst or an ingrown hair or an extraterrestrial's tracking device, all things that are more realistic

41

possibilities than that cancer-thing-that-other-people-get-and-it-never-happens-to-you disease.

They call my name, and I walk back through the door, alone. Every step I take, I am closer to understanding what this thing is. Closer to knowing that it's either cancer (which I know it is) or an alien GPS system (which it probably isn't but in many ways would be easier to deal with).

I jump up on that bed-table-thing with the giant roll of single-ply toilet paper covering it and glance around the room. There are no children's drawings. Instead there are just diagrams of penises and vaginas that go on and on, wall to wall. Dongs that have been split in half lengthwise to show me what the inside looks like. Uteruses and ovaries that resemble cow heads. Black arrows pointing to the dangly bits, informing me what is in my pants. A part of me wants to examine them closer, wants to read all the scientific jargon, but the other, louder side of me doesn't want to get caught staring at a drawing of a 16-inch schlong.

The door creaks, and Dr. Honda enters the room. He's a slim Asian man with a mustache and a big smile. He immediately makes me feel welcome and, as I will come to shortly learn, this is not a professional trait of all doctors. He has bedside manner, a characteristic and skill that cannot be taught.

He shakes my hand and introduces himself. He asks me a few questions about life, what do I do, am I married, do I have kids, where am I from, and then my pants are suddenly at my ankles yet again and I'm Porky-Piggin' it, naked from the waist down.

As he's squeezing my GPS tracking system with a rubber-gloved hand, I hear footsteps fast approaching in the hallway and quickly ask if the door is locked. He says they'll knock first. *Yeah*, I think, *But I'm sure it'll be that knock-knock-open that people are so wont to do.*

"My ultrasound guy is here today. I'm gonna have him check you out." I ask if I can pull up my pants.

You've read all this before. You know what happens. I know what happens. The story is inevitable.

I have Cancer.

That thing that makes people go bald and look sick and thin and tired. That thing that sucks the life out of individuals and kills kids and evaporates old folks. That thing I hear about on TV and in movies and sometimes in books. It's me. It's on me. It's in me. Growing. Slowly.

I picture it looking like the black goo that Venom is made out of in the popular *Spider-Man* films; it's not quite a gel but it's not quite a liquid.

It's just a mess of sticky tar that attaches and grows and builds and pulls and destroys until it has encompassed your very being and turned you into someone else. No more Peter Parker. No more Eddie Brock.

Venom.

Cancer.

I'm staring at the ceiling, cold jelly on my testicle. Now I know. Now I know that I was right. Everything I thought I knew was correct. My gut was dead on. Dead. On.

Dead.

Without looking at the Indian man who's given me my diagnosis, I ask, "Can I pull my pants up?" and he says, "Yes."

Pamphlets are spread out in front of me. Every single person on every single cover is happier than the last. Everyone is so *happy*. They're all so *happy* about their Cancer . . . and . . . I am just . . . .

. . . .

Dr. Honda tells me that I have two options in regard to the tumor. My Tumor. First, there is a surgery wherein they will cut me open and split my remaining testicle in half, removing the bad stuff but leaving me fertile. I tell him that I cannot fathom anything that sounds more painful. I ask him what the second option is.

He succinctly states, "Full removal."

I sigh and ask what the third option is. He stares back at me. Nobody says anything. After a moment he tells me that if they miss even one single cell during the nutcracker operation the cancer will simply return, and they'd have to perform a second surgery in order to take the remaining half. I assume this is supposed to make my decision easier.

I look at the ground. At my feet. At my pants. I tell him to take it all. He smiles, and it's a very kind face looking back at me. You can tell that he doesn't want to tell me these things. You can *see* his compassion, and I'm thankful for it.

He pokes the pamphlets and says, "You're going to want to bank your sperm," and I nod. I am going to be sterile. Unable to reproduce. There is something very damaging to me about this thought, and the memory of me lying in a hospital bed talking to a doctor when I am eight is at the forefront of my mind.

I shake his hand and walk out of his office. I walk down the hall. I walk back through the door and to my wife, surrounded by old people. She puts down her *Better Homes* magazine and stands up, smiles. We walk out of the office, down the steps and out the front door into the parking lot and the warm sunshine.

It has not crossed my mind how blissfully ignorant she currently is.

She looks at me and, with her complete confidence with the ingrown hair theory asks, "Well, what did he say?" and, without missing a beat, I respond, "I have a tumor."

She takes one more step before collapsing onto a parking block and begins weeping. This is when the reality all hits me, and I weep as well.

CHAPTER 6
PARENTS

Over the last few weeks I've left my parents in the dark because I didn't want to put them through unnecessary Cancer worry, especially if the problem were going to simply solve itself. Which it didn't. So now I have to work on The Big Reveal. And remember, as any good salesman will tell you, presentation is everything.

Jade pulls into a Walgreen's parking lot to buy a Diet Coke and we sit on the sidewalk and call her mom. "It's a lump. It's cancer. They're taking it, yes." My mother-in-law asks to speak to me. She asks me how I'm doing. She asks me how I'm feeling. I tell her that it's no big deal. I tell her that absolute very worst-case scenario is that I have to get a little chemotherapy, just some needle and I'll feel like I've got the flu for a bit. I'll get better. Whatever.

She says, "Wow." She says, "You're brave." She says, "Stay strong."

The truth is, I'm not brave. I'm being forced kicking and screaming through this scenario. I don't want to be here, and I never would have volunteered. I don't deserve this.

Deserve. That's an awfully big word that gets thrown around a lot. Maybe I do deserve it. I try to examine my life from a higher perspective. I've lied, cheated, and stolen; said hurtful things to people intentionally; torn people down verbally with complete purpose; and talked shit about my friends and family behind their backs. Maybe I do deserve this.

We drive home and I take a seat in my backyard on our patio furniture. I lean back in the chair and let the sun, one of the only absolute constants in our lives, hit my face, warm me, comfort me.

A man walks through my alley pushing a shopping cart and shouting, "*Tamale! Tamale! Tamale con queso!*" and I think about him and all my neighbors and how, as far as I know, none of them have cancer. Just me. Just all of a sudden. Nobody knows about my balls. Nobody anywhere knows or cares about anything right now.

My mom wanders around her home 1,500 miles away, feeding her dogs, her healthy children somewhere in the back of her head. My dad fixes a computer, thoughts of gigabytes and RAM clouding his brain, the world a dull fuzz outside of his peripheral.

Everything is about to change for them. They are about to become Parents Of A Child With Cancer.

I pick up the phone and call my mom first. I let it ring six times before I hang up. I set the phone down and stare at it, wondering if maybe she'll call right back. I stand up and start pacing, rubbing my thumb along the inside of my pinky, a nervous tick I have.

I pick up the phone again and try my dad. It rings twice before he answers in a distracted, gruffly voice. "This is Mike," he says. "Hey, Daaaaaad. It's me." I sort of let the word play out like that because I have no idea how to get into this conversation, how to ease into it; I didn't plan an opening act or monologue. "How's it going?" I ask, and he begins to tell me about computer problems that I don't and probably won't ever understand. I listen, but only to be polite because I didn't call to hear what he's been up to. I didn't call for any polite reason. I called with one intent and I'm just waiting for my selfish turn to speak.

"What's new with you?" he asks. And there's my window.

"Well," I say, struggling for the words, hoping that they would find me if I just started talking but . . . no. I throw eloquence and pacing to the wind and just say, "I have cancer."

There's a long pause on the other end like he's waiting for the punch line. The great joke this is bound to be. It doesn't come. Trust me, I'm still waiting myself.

He says, "Oh . . . kay . . . . Did you tell your mom?" and I say, "No," and he says, "You better let me tell her," and I quickly say, "NO! No . . . I'd

rather tell her myself," and he says, "Oh . . . kay . . . .
" and I quickly fill in the blanks with, "There's a good
chance I'll survive. I just . . . I have cancer . . . . "
There's more silence. Loads of it. Then he says,
"Your mom just got home. Why don't you call her?"
And I do.

"Yellow, John Boy! How ya' doin'?" My
mother is forever the chipper woman, her syllables
bouncing up and down playfully. I feel bad that I
have to destroy this. I say, "I'm doing good. I'm
doing OK. Did Dad talk to you?" and she, with a hint
of suspicion, says, "Nooo-ooooh. What's going on?"

I take a deep breath and shut my eyes. In my
head I think, *I'm sorry, Mom. I'm sorry. I wish I
didn't have to tell you this. I wish I could just keep it
from you and spare you and not drag you into it. I
wish I didn't have to damage you with this
information, and I'm sorry for the pain I'm about to
cause you.* I feel sick to my stomach.

"I have cancer."

Another long silence. I'll get used to these.
Like an old computer reading a large file, people need
a chunk of time to process a sizable piece of
information like that.

There are no tears. She doesn't cry.
Everything about this interaction is atypical. I tell her
I should survive and she says, "OK." I tell her I'll
keep her posted on everything and then, as she's

50

telling me goodbye, I hear her voice crack and I realize that she is first and foremost in shock, and second, trying to keep a straight face for my sake. I tell her goodbye and the moment I slam the phone closed I begin to cry, vicious sobs that wrench my body.

Moments later my phone rings, and I assume it's my mom calling back, but no. It's my brother-in-law, Jarod. I cover my eyes with the palm of my hand and wipe down, pushing the tears away. I look up at the sky, and I think about how there are people out there with real problems. People starving. People dying. *Currently* dying of cancer. Lung cancer. Heart cancer. Brain cancer. Get it together. I answer the phone, trying to sound cool but coming off like a mop. "Hey . . . . "

Jarod, three years my senior, says, "Heeeey. So I just heard about . . . . How are you doing?" and this is the one person I've spoken to so far who I don't want to cry in front of. This is my brother-in-law and the person I just want to shrug it off with and give an, "Eh, you know," but for some reason, I can't hold it back. Everything comes out. Everything I didn't tell my mom. Everything I didn't tell my dad. Everything I didn't tell my mother-in-law. Everything I didn't tell my wife. It comes out now.

Everything overflows.

"I'm so afraid. I'm so fucking afraid. I don't know what happened. I don't know how this

happened. I don't . . . I don't fucking deserve this *and . . . it's so fucked up. I can't have kids— I'm like some fucking . . . sterile . . . . I can't* fucking *have kids! And they're going to cut my nut off. I'm so afraid that I'm going to die. I don't want to die. I don't want to die."* And then I just cry into the phone and it feels so great and so terrible and Jarod says the absolute wisest thing he can.

Nothing.

He simply listens.

CHAPTER 7
MECHANICAL DONUT

For the past few days, I've been drinking a radioactive concoction called *barium* and trust me, there is neither anything *berry* or *yum* about it. Seventy-two hours ago, a small yellow package showed up at my front door postmarked from the hospital, asking that I mix this powder with water and drink deeply. How to describe it? So many competing tastes and textures. If I were being polite, I would say it has the consistency of semen swimming in powdered eggs (powdered lumps included) and tastes of Elmer's glue with just a hint of mint.

So no, it's not *terrible* but it is bad enough to make me plug my nose and gag while I try to chug it as quickly as possible lest flies mistake it for what it smells like and begin to lay eggs in it.

The chemical drink, I'm told, causes my insides to "light up" and reveal any inconsistencies with a "normal, healthy human," which, as far as I can tell, I am not. I'm not exactly sure what this procedure will be, but I assume they have some kind of machine that will take pictures of my insides; some kind of giant X-ray. I'm imagining lying on a bed and smiling; it's school photos all over again. THEN I'm imagining going across the street to Denny's because I saw that they're featuring their seasonal pumpkin pancakes right now, and I feel like I deserve a little comfort food.

A male nurse with black hair and a soul patch approaches me with a gown and says, "OK, Mr. Brookbank, we're going to get you in and out with your CAT scan. First, we'll have you put this gown on and then we'll get you all hooked up with your IV and blah blah blah." Everything else he says turns into static. My eyes shift to my wife, who grimaces. I say, "Uh . . . OK . . . OK. Do you . . . do you have a restroom I can change in and, uh . . . have a panic attack?" and the male nurse with the soul patch says, "Yes, absolutely. Right this way."

Inside the bathroom I change into the knee length, butt-revealing gown and stare at myself in the mirror; blue eyes filled with fear, wispy beard standing on end, skin the color of bad eggs. I don't give myself a pep talk. I don't say anything. I just stare at my reflection and try to imagine what it feels like to not be afraid of needles.

"Everyone is afraid of needles," my wife says and I respond with, "No. Nobody *likes* needles. Not everyone is *afraid* of them. I don't *like* the cold. I'm not *afraid* of it. You don't *like* onions. You're not *afraid* of them. My fear is deeply psychological and . . . it's very . . . you wouldn't understand. They're pointy and silver and . . . *They're just so fucking pointy and silver!*"

The Internet tells me the complex is called *trypanophobia*, an illness so foul that they actually had to give it a name no one could pronounce.

54

Soul Patch calls my name and escorts me into The Room. The door shuts and clicks behind me. In the middle of the floor is a giant Mechanical Donut, 6-and-a-half-feet high with a bed that rolls in and out of its delicious center. Next to the circular, steel pastry is a robotic arm that has a bag filled with clear liquid dangling from its "hand." It is this clear liquid, I understand without being told, that will be shot into my veins to assist and activate the barium.

I ask Soul Patch how long he's been doing this and he says, "Coupla' years," and I say, "I mean IVs. How long? Are you good at it?" and he says, "Oh. Yeah. Couple years. I'm good."

Yeah, right. Your voice has the confidence of an eighth grader buying beer. Intern! Intern! *Intern!* And for the first time I find myself intentionally trying to focus on the pulsating lump of my lump, trying to distract myself from the needle.

I ask him what the CAT scan is for, and he noncommittally answers, "Oh, you're a new patient, and we just like to do preliminary work on everyone prior to surgery," and I say, "But specifically my pelvis, abdomen, and lungs?" and he says, "Uh . . . yeah . . . sort of everywhere, but yeah. There, mostly," and I think, "Shame on you, kid. You're not old enough to buy beer and that *is* a fake ID." I think, "I know what you're looking for. You're looking to see if it's spread anywhere. You're looking to see if it's growing. You want to know what to do if the surgery doesn't work or if you're too late."

Soul Patch tells me to lie back and I do, reluctantly. He tells me to hold out my arm and I do, reluctantly. He holds my wrist and starts to slap around my forearm with two fingers. "How," he asks, "are your veins?" and I tell him I don't know. He asks if I've drunk any water recently and I say, "A little," and he says, "Uh, OK. This is usually a bit easier if you've been drinking water but we'll see what we can—" *slap, slap*—"do . . . . "

My eyes are the size of dinner saucers, and my hands curl into fists of fear. I want to scream for Jade to bring me water, water, *WATER!!!* A cup, a glass, a gallon, a hose, anything. *We'll see what we can do??!!* What does that mean?? I imagine him sliding the needle under my skin and into my vein, missing and probing, fishing, hooking, sticking, stabbing, wiggling, my wrinkled and hibernating vein exploding over and over, blood leaking out and running all over the floor. In my mind, Soul Patch keeps saying, "Oops, oops, sorry, again, once more, my bad," until I finally just pass out.

"There ya go." I look down, and it's done. He tells me to lie back and keep my arm with the silvery, pointy needle sticking in it above my head. "Keep it pointed at the ceiling," and I say, "The needle—is the needle still in my arm?" and he says, "Uh . . . no. It's just a small rubber hose," and I say, "Can I bend my arm without getting poked?" and he says, "Uh . . . yeah. I'll be in this room over here and I'll give you directions over the intercom." I try to bend my arm and feel a little poke. *Intern!* Or maybe it was just the

56

tape pulling at a hair. *I don't know.* But I bet that needle is still in there. In my arm. In my vein.

Soul Patch's voice comes over the intercom, and I turn my head to the left. He's in a booth that looks like it's being protected from radiation caused by nuclear fallout. I have to pause and wonder what sort of danger my body is currently in, what sort of rays I am about to endure. I try to remember what it was that *The Fantastic Four* were hit with when my train of thought is interrupted.

"Remember to keep your arm up—at the ceiling—like you have a question." The only question I have is, *When will this be over?*

I have no idea how unanswerable that actually is.

The tech, from his bomb shelter, says, "And here comes the dye." I watch the fluid come down the bag, through the tube, and into my arm, and then I'm pretty certain that I have legitimately shit my pants. Everything from my abdomen to my thighs is steaming hot.

The intercom comes back on. Soul Patch says, "The dye may cause you to feel like you've . . . wet . . . your pants," and I shut my eyes and take a deep breath, trying not to focus on the warmth in my pelvis.

The bed jerks and slides into the donut. I open my eyes and read a sign taped to the top of the donut hole: DO NOT LOOK DIRECTLY INTO THE LASER. A female robot voice comes through the donut, The Bakery God, and says, "Hold. Your. Breath." And I do. And I shut my eyes. And I pray. Not to the bakery god, but to That Faceless And Eternal Being. *I do not blame you. I do not understand. Help me.*

"You. May. Breathe." The robot says and the bed pulls me out of the donut sanctuary. "Doing OK?" Soul Patch asks, and I say, "Yeah," but in my head I think, *Not so great . . . . Did I shit my pants?*

The bed jerks forward again and the robot tells me, "Hold. Your. Breath."

What hangs in the balance of this test? What will these results reveal? The thought of this being the beginning of something bigger crosses my mind, and I try to push it away. For me, surgery is the end. There is a definitive *period* afterward, and I go home and go back to work and that's it but . . . .

What if . . . .

What if the cancer has spread? Lungs? Stomach? Liver? Is this possible? Yes. Yes, it's all definitely possible. But is it probable? I pause, trying to be logical and not emotional and yes, I realize, it is probable.

"You. May. Breathe."

58

Will I die in six months? *Could* I die in six months? I could die in six months. If it has spread, what are my chances for survival? The Internet tells me that, depending on what kind of cancer I have, it could be anywhere between 30 percent to 90 percent survival rate, which is basically like saying, "Maybe you'll die. Maybe you won't," and then shrugging unapologetically.

"Hold. Your. Breath."

CHAPTER 8
HAVING A BALL

Like all good hospitals, ours made us wait the *entire* weekend before giving us the (maybe) life-changing results of our test. Over those three days, every stomachache turned into stomach cancer, every pain in my finger exploded into bone cancer, every headache transformed into brain cancer. By the time they called back late Monday afternoon, I had diagnosed myself as a tumor wearing clothes.

"What are my results? My, uh, my test results?" and the lady on the phone says, "I'm not allowed to give out that information, sir," and I say, "I know. I know you're not. But it's OK. It's me, er, my body. It's my body. It's not a secret to me," and she says, "I just really can't, and actually, I just don't have access to the information. The doctor would, however, like to speak with you."

Outside, thunder claps and lightening strikes and the camera zooms dramatically into my face and I hear the soundtrack of my life play dun-DUN-*DUUUUUUN!!!*

I take a half-day off work the next day and drive back to Arcadia to visit with Dr. Honda, the friendly neighborhood urologist. When I arrive, all the receptionists know me by name and smile and welcome me in and everything is just too friendly. Jade and I sit down and she picks up the same copy of

Better Homes she'd been reading previously and opens up to the page she had habitually dog-eared.

A woman calls my name and both my wife and I stand up. I start walking forward while Jade casually slides the magazine into her purse. The receptionist leads us back through a narrow corridor crowded by old people with various urinating issues. We take a seat in the room where I was told I had cancer and Jade says, "Is this where he told you?"

And I say, "Yes."

And she says, "Where were you sitting?"

And I say, "Here."

And she says, "And was he right here?"

And I say, "Yes."

And she says, "Did you cry?"

And I say, "No. I said, 'Rats.'"

She glances suspiciously around before sliding out her hot copy of *Better Homes* just before Dr. Honda knock-knock-enters. Jade shoves the magazine back in her purse like she's just been caught trying to purchase extra-tiny condoms. The doctor shakes my hand, and I introduce him to my wife. He smiles and says, "Nice to meet you," and takes a seat.

To his right, he sets down a regular manila envelope with my name scratched onto the tab. Inside that envelope, I think, is everything. My future is just out of my reach.

He makes small talk with me and asks how my job is going, and I answer in short but courteous statements. He finally says, "Welp!" and grabs the folder and opens it on his lap and here comes The News.

"You have," and he slides his finger down the page, turns it, examines the second page, "stage one cancer."

I drop to my knees and tear my shirt and wail and scream and curse the Earth and the doctor says, "That's . . . uh . . .that's the kind we already knew you had," and I immediately sit back on the paper-covered table and compose myself and say, "That's great!"

Dr. Honda says, "It hasn't spread. We'll do the surgery and that should be it."

"*YES!*" We are going to (literally) cut this villain off at the pass and bury it alive. Goodnight, dickwad!

"Just out of curiosity," I ask, "How high do the stages go?" and the doctor says, "Four. They go to four."

CHAPTER 9
DR. CHAPLIPS

Another doctor's office. Another Georgia O'Keeffe painting. The sun beats in through a west-facing window, and I think the AC must be broken. My wife holds my hand. Am I sweaty? Is she clammy? I can't tell. The thumb of my free hand rubs the denim of my jeans. I try to concentrate on the fabric to pass the time until—

The door opens and a man in a knee-length lab coat enters. He sits down across from us and the very first thing I take in about him (after the lab coat) is that his lips are in*credibly* chappy. Not just Chapstick chappy but I've-been-lost-in-the-desert-for-two-weeks-was-rescued-and-came-right-to-work chappy. White, dead skin juts at all angles like shards of milky, broken glass. His little pink tongue keeps darting out and licking them like a weasel gathering eggs, and I'm fairly confident that he's simply eating the dusty flakes.

Oh my goodness, I can't stop staring. It's like a woman with her cleavage exposed. I *want* to look you in the eyes. I genuinely do. But your tig ol' bitties are boring directly into my soul.

He shakes my hand, and I make a note to wash it the first chance I get. He welcomes us to the clinic. He explains to us what The Process will look like.

IVF.

In vitro fertilization.

Or . . . How To Make Babies With Science. Petri dishes, egg retrievals, frozen sperm. That sort of thing.

"The first step," he says, "is to do a semen analysis. We need to see where your numbers are," and I look at Jade and then back at his incredibly disgusting lips. I say, "Uh . . . OK. What does that . . . entail?" and he explains that I simply have to masturbate into a cup. Simply right now. Simply in public. It's all very simple.

I cough into my hand but quickly pull it back, realizing that's the one I shook his with and now most likely contains some sort of lip contagion. I look at my wife and I look at my feet and I look at the Georgia O'Keeffe vagina painting and I say to the doctor in the most, "*Liiiiiiiiisten*," type of way possible, "I, uh . . . actually. I actually just, uh . . . masturbated . . . this morning and I'm not sure . . . I'm not sure I'm going to be able to really, frankly, hammer another one out today," and he says, "You'll be fine," and my wife says, "You'll be fine," and the doctor says, "She can help," and my exit strategies have all been blocked off. These two perverts are going to force me at gunpoint to tug my leather tether.

He escorts us into another, larger room, filled with worker bees buzzing around with papers and

66

folders. The three of us approach a desk together and the doctor tells the young woman sitting in her swivel chair that I need a semen analysis done and she is just so very, very, professional. She just says, "OK," and he says, "It might be slightly lower than usual because he just masturbated this morning," and no one even acknowledges how bizarre this statement is. What a strange place this must be to work! I just look down at my hands. My dirty, dirty, masturbating hands.

The doctor shakes my hand (gross) and tells me, "Good luck," and he walks away, probably to eat an aloe vera plant.

The woman behind the desk hands me a cup and says, "Back through that door on the right. No lubrication. No spit," and she looks directly at my wife and I say, "Oh . . . *Ooooooh* . . . . "

We walk through the appropriate door and find ourselves in a room roughly the size of a hotel conference hall. Everything is white. Everything is sterile. The fluorescents buzz in the ceiling. On the walls: Georgia O'Keeffe.

Of course.

Sitting next to the door is a small table cluttered with *Sports Illustrated Swimsuit Editions*. Motivation. In the center of the room is a chair that can only be described as something you would get a root canal in. It's black, leather, and constantly at a slight recline. I sit in it and assume that this specific posture has been scientifically proven to help nervous men climax in public places.

"How do we . . . " I begin to say and my wife laughs at the sudden and absolute absurdity of our lives. She says, "I don't know!" as she unzips my pants and gives, what can only be considered, her best. As long as that little power ring is on her third finger, I know that she is my sidekick through everything.

I stare at the ceiling, at the fluorescent lights. Everything is so bright. To my left are Venetian blinds leading outside where I can see passersby meandering to and fro. I look at the door 25 feet away from me and ask Jade if it's locked. She says yes and continues with her medical chore. *Tug-yank-jerk.*

The lights buzz. The receptionists chat. Phones ring. People pass by. My tumor throbs. I ask Jade to stop and she says, "Why? Are you close?" and I say, "No. I think my dick skin is starting to look like that doctor's lips," and she laughs and says, "Oh, my gosh! I couldn't stop staring! They were so *flakey*! Did he just come from the desert?" and then I laugh and she squeezes into the chair with me.

We kiss and try to be cute and romantic but then I say, "I'm telling you . . . this morning . . . " and Jade says, "NO!" like it's a personal challenge to milk venom from the snake. She goes back to town, and I bite my bottom lip but not in that sexy way that girls do it but more in that way where I'm trying to focus through the pain. Where is my power animal? I picture a lamb screaming.

I shut my eyes and imagine any number of perverse sexual acts but they all end with my dick being shoved into a meat grinder and lit on fire.

Finally, in a mode of complete desperation, I grab the wheel in one hand and her tit in the other. I put my mind into Zen mode and focus on success and focus on success and focus on suck sex.

I'll skip the rest of the details but suffice it to say that this tale ends with me spraying a pathetic amount of jizz into a plastic cup. There is no clean way to say that. Romance of the twenty-first century, baby.

Covered in sweat and shame, we exit the room and approach the receptionist from earlier.

She knows. Oh, she knows.

"Everything go OK?" she asks, and I tell her that a little mood lighting could go a long way. She smiles and hands me a receipt. She asks me to sign and I say, "You need the ol' John Han*cock*, huh?" and she laughs and the woman next to her laughs and a guy a couple yards away laughs and suddenly everything is all right. We're all humans and we all know how awkward this is and we all try our best to be professional.

I sign my name and limp away.

CHAPTER 10
TRY, TRY AGAIN

Like many people, my wife and I have always wanted kids. The problem, however, with having kids is that you actually have to *have* them. You actually have to say to yourself, "Today is the day that I'm going to *try* to have a kid. Today is the day that I'm going to throw all protection to the wind and *go for it*. It's a big decision that no one should make lightly or while under the influence of alcohol, hard drugs or cancer.

My wife asks me, "Do you want to have kids?"

And I say, "Of course."

And she says, "When?"

And I say, "When I'm done dying."

She considers this answer and then tries a new angle, "I've been thinking . . . " and I know her sentence isn't over so I just wait. "I've been thinking that maybe we should . . . try now."

I look at my watch even though I'm not wearing one. I push the hair out of my eyes, even though I don't have any. I cough into my hand even though there's nothing in my throat and I say, "Now now or now later?" and she says, "My *clock* says now now would be the best time." She says, "What if . . .

what if we just get pregnant now? Naturally? And we can do that together and experience that together and just . . . . "

It's the first time I realize how much she loves me. Cancer isn't just affecting *me*. It's affecting *her*. And not just in the way that proximity calls for, either. If she wants to be with me, stay married to me, and still have kids, she's going to have to go through the very invasive process of in vitro fertilization, which, for her, is going to consist of so much more than spunking into a cup: hormones, shots, surgeries, egg retrievals. While I get to look at porno in a room by myself, she has to be probed by a group of strangers.

I stand up and give her a hug and look her in the eyes and try to make the moment seem like something I saw in a movie but it's simply not because we both know the reality. We both know that I'm dying. Or could die. Or might die. Or might survive. We both know that we know nothing. We both know that this is all we know. Each other. Doctors and medicines and surgeries are about to invade our lives and this is all we can control. Each other. Right now.

I say, "OK," and I'm certain.

And then we're in the bedroom and there is so much pressure on me to perform that it is a complete failure, and I should go to summer school or read the CliffsNotes on sex or SOMETHING. It's so bad that I have to apologize and stop. All I can think about is a ticking clock, and I don't know if that clock is my life or her cycle, and I can just feel my tumor throbbing, and I just keep having an image of spraying out black venom, octopus ink instead of white semen. I know that's disgusting and I apologize but it's all I can think about.

I never share the image with Jade.

A few hours later we try again and the next day we try again and the next afternoon and the next night and the next day and again and again and again and sometimes it works and sometimes it doesn't and why are my hands so sweaty?

It's midnight and Jade tells me she wants to buy a pregnancy test. She tells me she thinks she might be pregnant and . . . I'm so excited. We're so excited. This is it—that ray of hope, of sunshine, of light in the dark storm. Something that is ours. We drive to the local drug store and buy a pee test and a Diet Coke.

She chugs it like a frat boy and whizzes on the stick. We wait for the longest seven minutes of our lives. We stand in the bathroom, staring at the test, waiting for the blue line to appear or not appear or is it a plus sign or why do they make these things so hard to read?

Something starts to come through . . . and it looks like she's pregnant!! We're squeezing hands but not saying anything and then . . . the weird symbol fades and we let go of each other and stare at the blank stick and shake it a bit and try to read the directions again: 1. Pee on stick. 2. Wait. Check and check.

We try again and the same thing happens. We ultimately decide that maybe she's pregnant (YAY!) but not pregnant *enough* (understandable). So we just keep having as much sex as we can and peeing on sticks every couple days, and ultimately, she isn't pregnant, and I have to start cryobanking my semen in three days and that's it. Game over. We won't be getting pregnant The Old-Fashioned Way. If we want it, we'll have to pay $12,000 for it. If we want it, we'll have to find a clinic and hire a doctor and go through procedures and hope and pray and leave it in the hands of others. Anger rises up in both of us. That anger that shouts, "It's not fair!" and it isn't. But it doesn't care. Whatever "it" is.

It's not fair that every drunk jackass can accidentally impregnate his girlfriend and it's not fair that people are throwing their babies away and having abortions and leaving them behind dumpsters and flushing them down toilets and I know one guy who has 22 kids with 14 different women, and I want to approach him and stick a knife in his throat for hogging all the good karma.

All I want doesn't matter.

CHAPTER 11
BABY BLOCKS

Three hundred million: That is both the amount of money *Forrest Gump* made theatrically, as well as the average number of human sperm per serving, according to *Wikipedia*.

Fifty-six: the yearly average number of people on the Sioux Falls, South Dakota, bowling league, as well as the number of healthy sperm in my semen analysis, according to Dr. Chaplips, whom I currently have on the phone.

I ask him what the chances are of me getting my wife pregnant. I hear him lick his lips and, judging by the crackling noise coming through the line, I assume he still hasn't solved his oral issue. "Aaahh," he says. "Almost impossible. Very unlikely." I say, "One thousand to one?" and he pauses before saying, "Probably higher."

"Higher? Like what? What are my chances of a standard human pregnancy?" I don't know why I'm doing this to myself. I don't know why I'm asking these questions. It's already too late to do anything about it because the cryobank suggests that I *abstain from myself* for three days previous to each deposit. I just feel this desire to know how defective I am. If I were a term paper, what grade would I receive?

"Probably more around one hundred thousand to one."

I take a couple small breaths and ever the *Dumb and Dumber* enthusiast, say, "So you're telling me there's a chance?" He's clearly never seen the movie because he just says, "No. I'm not." I thank him and hang up. I tell my wife the great news. "Babe," I say, "We never, ever, *ever* have to use condoms again! Don't you get it? I'm as sterile as a crayon! A potato has more potential for reproduction than I do! This is fantastic! This—this sucks . . . . "

Inside I can feel the growth, the landmass, the intruder, the Cancer, growing larger and larger on my testicle. Every moment of every day I am reminded of it. Every moment of every day, I have a constant throbbing pain. Every day it grows and grows and grows. What was once a tiny pea is now a lima bean. It's getting bigger. It's stretching out. It's making itself at home. And still I can do nothing. If I want to bank what little functioning sperm I have, there is nothing to do but wait. If I want children, I must gamble with my life. True Russian roulette.

The pain grows and the doctor prescribes me Vicodin, which I begin to pop like Tic Tacs or cashews or addictive prescription drugs. The pain grows more and I pop more Vicodin and the pain grows more and I pop more Vicodin and the pain grows more and I wait and wait and wait to bank. The banking will take a month. The banking will take

76

thirty days. Cancer will take full advantage of me in that time, feeding itself and fueling itself off me.

The waiting gives me anxiety, and I neurotically touch My Lump, the way people will continue to play with a hangnail or tongue the sore spot in their mouth. My body wants it out, and I'm forcing it to stay in. My body hates me, and I am sorry.

Call me selfish. Call me crazy. Call me reckless. But I'll have my children.

Even if it kills me.

Fast forward a couple blurry days, and I'm taking the Olympic Boulevard exit off the 405 freeway at 8 a.m. I've got my first appointment scheduled with the sperm bank this morning and am very excited to open a savings account with them.

The building is tucked away and is fairly understated, causing me to drive around the block a couple times before I find it. The parking lot only holds about eleven cars and most of the spaces are empty. On the front door is an intercom switch. I hit the button and wait. Someone buzzes me in.

Hidden buildings, hi-tech locks, espionage! This is getting dead sexy, and I've seen enough James Bond movies to know that the chicks involved are going to be *hot*. I open the door and put on my "cool face," expecting to see some smoking bombshell blonde in a short nurse's skirt. In my head, she looks just like the girl on the cover of Blink 182's *Enema of the State* album. Those clowns at the semen analysis place don't know shit about shit, making me rub one out in a dentist chair. These people here are professionals. I have no doubt about that. Professionals. Hot Nurses. Hot Nurse Professionals.

I cup my hand over my mouth, smell my breath, and walk into a reception area containing only six chairs. An older gentleman who arrived before me lowers his newspaper and glances at me through Coke-bottle glasses. We make eye contact and both immediately think, *You're here to jack off!* and then, *JINX! 1-2-3-4-5-6-7-8-9-10!*

He lifts his paper back up, and I turn my attention to the Hot Nurse Station where I come face to face with Bill Cosby and Mimi from *The Drew Carey Show*. The first sits behind an ancient IBM whose white plastic sheen has turned the color of eggnog, while Mimi digs through towering filing cabinets twice her height.

Now it should be noted that these two people are not *actual* Bill Cosby and not *actual* Mimi from *The Drew Carey Show* but individuals who look so incredibly similar that they could be hired to work at a children's birthday party as cheap duplicates.

One final word on their characters: I will describe the first person as both "Bill Cosby" and then as "she" but trust me when I say that both of these descriptors are not only accurate, they are also absolutely necessary.

Bill Cosby says, "License, please," and I slide my ID over the counter. Without looking up, she says, "Is this your current address?" and I say, "No. I didn't drive *that* far." She looks at me sideways, and I say, "It's a South Dakota license."

She glances back at it and laughs far harder than is deemed even remotely necessary for what can only be considered a subpar joke. She then repeats her folly to her coworker, Mimi, in a fit of giggles. Mimi says, "What? You're laughing too hard. I can't understand," and so Bill repeats it again, the poor joke becoming less and less funny with every turn.

"Riiiiiight . . . . Buzz him in," Mimi commands and Bill Cosby opens a door, ushering me to The Back. He/she hands me a small cup—sort of the ATM deposit envelope, if you will—and then says, "Choose any door on your right." I examine each of them in turn and discover that they all look identical save for room 4, which has been decorated with wallpaper adorned with silhouettes of naked women.

I choose the room I'm standing in front of. I figure it's the closest to reception and therefore probably the least used. Only a true pervert would choose this room, so close to other people. Only a true sicko would choose—I stop analyzing my choice.

Bill Cosby hands me a disc. I look at it: an adult DVD artfully titled *Bangin' at the Cabo Cabana*. I say, "Thank you," and he/she turns and walks away.

I enter the room and shut the door. Lock the door. This is not what I expected on the drive over. It's a 4 x 4 closet with a 7" flat screen television and a stack of hardcore, full penetration, tit-squishing, spread-'em-wide, take-no-prisoners, anything goes, pornographic magazines.

I flip through a couple, and the pages are genuinely stuck together, crusty with usage. The classic joke isn't that funny when you find your fingers running over a stranger's dried semen. I drop the magazines and pop in the DVD. At this point, I'm still not certain if I'm going to watch it to the end. I'm not sure how I feel about this, making children like this. "Son, I remember the day I ejaculated you. I was in a closet by myself, watching a Puerto Rican girl get sandwiched by a couple of brothers who kept high-fiving."

Curiosity being what it is, I hit play and turn the volume down. There is a pair of headphones connected to the television but I have no desire to touch them, let alone put them on my head. I wait. And then it begins. The most horrific thing I could imagine begins. From the sky, eight individual baby blocks drop until they're in the middle of the screen. On each block is a letter and, all of them together spell out the name of the production company, which

I won't name here, a production company that, obviously, specializes in making porno strictly for sperm banks.

Everything really has been thought of. Half of me is disgusted and half of me applauds their ingenuity and sense of entrepreneurial pioneering. Actually, half and half is an unfair ratio. I'll call it a 90/10 split, respectively.

And then, just like that, without any set up or story, without someone entering a room or taking off their clothes, without any dialogue or foreplay, from frame numero uno, *Bangin' at the Cabo Cabana* immediately earns its title.

I reach up and hit stop. The screen goes black again. Much like the girl in the video, I feel as though I've gotten my fill of Hector (my name for the male actor), and I'm really concerned that if I watch the video to the end, the guy, rather than choosing to go with the "traditional" adult ending, will just decide to neatly collect his "product" in a little plastic vial and then set it on a nearby counter and frankly, if that happens, I believe I would just go limper than a spaghetti noodle in a bubble bath.

Mimi and Bill Cosby stop outside my door to chat about a party this weekend, some kind of dinner date. Mimi has a bad cough, full of phlegm. Bill Cosby does most of the talking and laughing. I double check to make sure the door is locked.

I'm so ashamed to be here. Not that I'm ashamed that I have cancer or that I'm sterile. I'm just feeling these very powerful emotions of human shame about masturbating. I can only equate it to pooping in the woods. You know it's OK. You know everyone that you're with is doing it and it's totally normal but you're just afraid someone is going to come around the corner and catch you in your most exposed state.

Snap out of it, Brookbank! I yell at myself. *You're paying* them *to be here! Now pull out that dick, and get yer whack on!*

I do. And with the help of those sticky-paged magazines and the blonde cop with the nightstick on p. 27, it takes considerably less time then the dentist's reclining chair experience did. I'm not really going to get into the logistics of the deposit itself, but I will say this: Even after my final visit, I'm *still* not completely certain what the best way to get the "money" from my "wallet" into the "envelope" is.

Once the deed is done, I screw the yellow lid on and it's only then that I realize that they've never told me what to do with it. At the semen analysis place there was a Mr. Ed style half-door that I opened and placed the jar into to be gathered up by a faceless technician in the next room. I search the walls. Nothing.

I put my pants back on (yes, I felt the strange need to remove them completely, as the only thing that could make this a bit more awkward is dried cum gracing the cover of my jeans), unlock the door and slowly, *slowly* open it. I don't want to alert anyone that I'm done. More shame. Shame. Shameful Shaming Shame!

Should I leave my cum basket behind? Should I take it with me? Which is the least horrendous situation: the one where I abandon it in the room and a stranger finds it, or the one where I'm caught in the hallway trouncing around with a porno snack pack?

After weighing the pros and cons endlessly, I decide to plant the plastic container into my palm and sort of twist my hand backward so that no approaching person will see what I'm carrying. I walk through a small labyrinth of narrow hallways up to another counter with more bulletproof glass, and I stop to wonder how many times sperm banks have been robbed. I set my collection of human sperm down on the counter and ring a bell. *DING!* ATTENTION EVERYONE IN THE GENERAL VICINITY! THIS YOUNG MAN HAS JUST COMPLETED HIS JACK OFF! CONGRATULATIONS, SIR!

I turn to leave and *almost* make it back to the exit when a small Asian woman who looks like Michelle Kwan wearing a baggy blue hazmat suit (helmet and all) pops her head out from the sliding glass door and says in a Darth Vadery voice, "Excuse me . . . sir . . . . " All these dots are where Darth is doing his heavy breathing. "I need to ask you . . . a few questions . . . . "

I come back over to Darth Kwan and, with my canned specimen resting next to her writing hand, she says, "How long . . . have you been . . . absent . . . ?" and I just assume she means abstinent.

She says, "Did you get it all . . . in the cup?"

I want to tell her that most of it went on the floor because of their stupid little cup technology. I want to tell her it's on the TV and all over the magazines and on the headphones. I want to tell her that someone needs to go in there with some baby wipes and give every object in that room a cursory once-over.

But I don't. Instead I just nod and say, "Yes, ma'am. It was a clean escape."

At the front desk they charge me a hundred bucks and I say, "A hundred bucks? But I did all the work!" and ol' Bill Cosby certainly thought THAT one was funny. And I don't blame him/her.

CHAPTER 12
TIME OFF

I've been banking "successfully" for several weeks now. Every Monday and Thursday, I come into work feeling like a completely twisted weirdo. My producer asks me how my morning is, and I turn to him, a guy I call Cookie Dave, and say, "Cookie Dave, this morning I jacked off into a cup inside of a commercial business. If I'm being totally honest with you, the last couple weeks have been pretty strange." He hands me a small napkin with a cookie in it and asks if I'd like it. "Thank you." Peanut butter. My favorite.

He asks me how the whole "cancer thing" is going, and I say, "They're going to cut out my ball in a few days. They're going to just . . . cut it out completely," and he says, "Ouch," and takes another bite.

"Yes," I say. "Ouch," I repeat. Cookie Dave tells me to call him when I'm done with my edit, and he exits just as my boss walks into my bay and begins telling me about some zombie movie he recently saw. I try to listen, but his words all run together into a sonic blur. He says, "Dead," he says, "Blood," he says, "Tumor," and I say, "What?" and he says, "*TWO MORE! They're making two more sequels!*" *a*nd I say, "I have cancer," and he sits down on my couch and says, "What?"

I try to explain it in the most succinct way possible. "I felt a lump on my nuts . . . . I went to the doctor . . . . I have cancer."

"Uh . . . uh . . . " he stammers. This speech pattern and the blank looks and the blind stares and the hopeless get-well-soon phrases are something to which I'll shortly become accustomed. He looks at me like I'm a puppy that's had its hind legs blown off and now rolls around in one of those sort of cute, sort of depressing doggy wheelchairs. "Well . . . uh . . . that sucks." "Yes," I say. "It does suck. I have surgery in a couple days and they're going to try to remove it. I need some time off," and he says, "Yes! Yes! Absolutely! Anything you need! Any time off you need, you take it!" And then, again, "That sucks, man. That really . . . sucks."

The room is silent, and I feel my tumor throbbing, calling out to me, begging for attention. I sniff and rub my nose, not crying, just trying to make noise to break the horrible silence. He says, "Wow," and I say, "This zombie movie . . . . It's good?" and he says, "They *run!*"

The throbbing continues and the black venom stretches out slowly into my body while I do nothing but wait.

CHAPTER 13
SURGERY

We drive to the hospital on a Friday morning for my out-patient surgery. I always assumed that, when the time finally came, I would be considerably more depressed or mournful. But instead, there is a freedom that is both liberating and intoxicating in the air. I'm just happy that this will soon be over. Today.

Take my nut. Just save my life. Take the poison before it spreads.

As I sit in the waiting room, no thoughts of hormone supplements cross my mind. The word *eunuch* never enters my brain. The only thing I can think about right now, the only impending doom I can imagine, the enormous, inevitable snowball that's rushing toward the small village that is my psyche, is the thought of the IV.

But, thankfully, I tell myself, it's the last one for a long, long time. "Just get through this one and you're good. You're gold. You can do it."

On the television in the waiting room is a talk show where the special guest is a young musician speaking about coffee enemas. I stand up and turn the TV off just as a nurse calls my name.

My testicle leaps nervously into my stomach and it feels like it's trying to give me one last hug. I say, "I hate goodbyes," but it won't let go.

The nurse leads my wife and I into a cream-colored room and instructs me to put on The Gown. When I come out of the bathroom, dressed for surgery, she's ready to stick me with the IV and for some reason I feel like this is The Line. I feel as though, at any point before the IV, I was free to turn around and run away and lead a life anyway I chose, but the IV . . . . It represents a kind of umbilical cord to the hospital. Like red vests at Wal-Mart—they make it very easy to differentiate between who belongs here and who doesn't.

I tell the nurse that I'm afraid of needles and she just laughs and I lean forward and say, "No, listen. I'm *afraid.* Do you have a numbing shot? I've heard that such a thing exists." And she says, "A shot before the shot?" and I say, " . . . Yes," and she says, " . . . Sure."

The nurse excuses herself to get the pre-numbing needle and returns with a freaking golden retriever! Bedside manner, ladies and gentlemen. The extra mile.

I say, "What the H-E-C-K is this!?" and the nurse says, "This is Samantha. She's our therapy dog. We let children pet her before they get shots—I mean patients—we let all patients of every age pet her before they get shots."

I say, "I see," and stare into Samantha's eyes while I lie back. They're a beautiful brown, almost golden color, and I hand my arm to The Extra Mile Nurse and Samantha pants and smells my right hand and The Extra Mile nurse taps my left forearm. Samantha says, "Don't worry, kid, everything is going to be all right because I love you just for being you," and I say to The Extra Mile Nurse, "Don't forget the numbing needle," and she says, "Of course," and I feel a poke and I look deep down into Samantha's eyes while I hold my breath and I wonder how many hundreds and thousands of children this dog has been loved by, how many eyes have stared directly into hers. I wonder where she sleeps at night and how she's treated.

"All done," The Extra Mile Nurse says and I say, "I only felt one poke," and she says, "I know; the numbing shot worked!" and I look over on the table and only see the remains of a single syringe.

The Extra Mile Nurse turns to leave and pats her leg and takes Samantha with her, and I feel my hand run down her head, down her back, down her tail, and she's gone.

I never see either of them again.

Later, another, younger nurse comes in and tells me that she's here to give me a "cocktail." She says it will help take the edge off and make me a little sleepy. I ask her where she was twenty minutes ago.

She plugs a bag into my IV and I . . . take . . . a nap . . . .

Minutes or hours or days have passed. I wake up, and I'm still in the same room. I feel my crotch. My testicle is still there. My tumor is still there. For a true moment, I was hoping they had pulled a quick one on me and had it all done with.

The Young Nurse comes back in, tells me that it's time to go, and takes me away. Two more nurses meet her in the hallway and the three of them navigate me through wide, bright, green corridors. I watch the overhead lights wash over me and try to remember every movie I've ever seen that uses that shot. I listen to the wheel on my gurney squeak.

This is it.

They push me around a corner, and I sit up and look over my shoulder and wave to my wife. She waves back and shouts, "Good luck! I love you! I love you!" and then I'm all alone, surrounded by scrubs.

They push me through a set of double doors and into a large room that smells like rubbing alcohol. Two women help me slide from my bed onto another bed. No—this isn't a bed. This is an operating table. I'm on The Slab.

I lie back and stare at the ceiling, where a gigantic light on a rotating arm hangs above me. A pretty young lady with red hair leans down over me and says, "Are you comfortable?" and I adjust my shoulders and say, "Yes," and she says, "Good." She says, "I'm going to inject you with something. Is that all right?" and I say, "Is this—is this the stuff that's going to put me down?" and she laughs as her thumb slowly pushes on the plunger, and there is an explosion in my chest that rises into my mouth that tastes like copper. I lick my lips and say, "See you on the—"

Other side.

When I wake up moments later I find myself sick and wanting to vomit. An oxygen mask covers my face. I try to sit up and look around because I have this feeling of complete nakedness. Not of *nudeness*, not the sensation of being unclothed, but of being exposed and out of place. I can only equate it to the feeling I get when I suddenly find myself walking through the young teen's bra section at Target. *What—how did I get here? I hope no one sees me— where's the exit? Run! No, don't run, you'll look suspicious. Walk slowly—no, not* that *slowly, you'll look like you're perusing. Just keep moving.*

I look to my right and see a row of hospital gurneys that are all empty and I suddenly feel a sense of impending doom, like I'm the next and final victim in some mad science experiment.

Why do I taste pennies?

My throat hurts fiercely. I bring up my hand to rub my trachea and see that there's a tube taped to my forearm. Oh, yeah. Everything hits me in a quick wave: Cancer. Hospital. Testicle. I remember why I'm here, what I'm doing. I lie down and hold back my gag reflex. The only thing worse than being in the bra section at Target is puking there.

Suddenly, a nurse is standing above me but I don't remember what she looks like or how old she was. She asks how I'm doing, and I tell her that it feels like I'm burping up pennies. She laughs and asks if she can touch my beard. I have to pause and reflect if she's having a bad day and needs a therapy dog like Samantha to help her through it. I willingly tilt up my chin and she runs her fingers through my face pubes.

She tells me that she thinks I might be Amish—a remark I get often thanks to the pattern in which my beard naturally grows; two long side burns into a neck beard thing I call The Hanging Tomato Plant. Hair simply refuses to grow on my cheeks or upper lip.

I tell her I'm not Amish, as far as I know, but secretly wish I were, which is true. I tell her my throat really is sore and she tells me it's because they stuck a tube down it and I ask if they used a hammer to get the job done.

I shift my eyes to the left and have a quick daydream. I suddenly see my naked, flaccid body on a slab. I see a tube shoved down my throat. I see eight people standing around me, cutting me, sucking my blood into machines, moving my penis and pulling my testicle out through a hole in my abdomen; a male C-section. I see the tumor, a big black pulsating alien brain connected to veins leading back into my cavity. I see them cauterize the wound. I see scissors and sutures. And I see this nurse, standing next to me, holding my penis up with a gloved hand to keep it out of the way of danger.

My eyes shift back to the right.

After what The Faceless Nurse deemed an acceptable length of time, someone wheels me downstairs to a second recovery room where they prop me into a recliner that I swear was the softest chair I'd ever, *ever* been in.

A new nurse, a chubby blonde woman in her late fifties, gives me some crackers and apple juice, and I'm certain she was probably a kindergarten teacher at some point and is just role-playing with me.

I tell her I feel sick, hoping to get some kind of high-powered-hospital-quality medicine that is going to take away these waves of nausea, but instead, she brings me a bed pan shaped liked an old man's kidney.

Gee, thanks. You shouldn't have.

She takes one step back and I puke three times; acidy strings of yellow and white saliva get stuck in my beard. The Teacher Nurse says, "Are you Amish?" and I wipe my chin on my sleeve and hand her the kidney. She says, "You should probably just keep that."

Over her shoulder, I see my wife enter the room and, thank you, thank you, thank you, I'm no longer alone. I'm no longer scared or afraid. It's just her and me and that's it. She says, "Gross! You puked! In front of everyone!" and I laugh.

She hands me a real-life cactus that has been decorated with construction paper flowers and adorned with various Game Boy cartridges. At my heart, I am a stupid little vomiting boy.

I say, "Thank you. This is very nice. I'm going to puke again," and she says, "OK," and takes the flowers from me. I grab the defiled bedpan and hold the rank and frothy mixture up to my mouth. I heave once, twice, and then puke doesn't come up but instead some kind of salty cracker concoction. When I look up I see both my wife and The Teacher Nurse staring at me. I look to my left and see another older nurse that I hadn't registered before watching me, as well. Where were these people coming from? Did they hear there was going to be a show? I politely ask them all why they're staring at me and each of them, in turn, looks down at their feet.

I stare back into my bedpan and can feel all three sets of eyes slowly rise up, waiting, watching, anticipating me, each of them so excited to watch me erupt. "*Oh, yes,*" they are surely thinking, "*Here he goes—his breathing is getting heavy! This is going to be amazing!*"

Nothing comes out and there is a collective sigh. Sorry to disappoint. I tell The Teacher Nurse that I have to go to the bathroom and she says, "Number one or number two?" and then I'm positive that I'm stuck in some weird role-play with her. I say, "Uh, I just sort of have to pee," and she says, "OK, that's number one. Let me help you up, sweetie."

I hobble across the floor with a 4-foot, 2-inch, fifty-something year old woman "supporting" me. Her perfume is pungent. She opens a door, and I mumble my thanks before shutting it and opening my robe and this is the first time that I realize I'm wearing some kind of—I don't really know the best way to describe it—a *nut-sack diaper*, I guess.

It's like a jock strap with no cup.

I exit the bathroom and excitedly ask the nurse if I get to keep my new accessory and she says, with an air of English dignity, "It's called a scrotal support. And yes, it's yours to keep." The best gift a boy could ask for. I say, "It's perfect. You're so sweet. You shouldn't have."

The Teacher Nurse helps me back to my chair where I find a doctor handing a folder to my wife. He says, "I don't know what you're going to do with them, but we took 'em," and Jade smiles and says, "Thanks," and the doctor says, "From what I could tell, we got it in time and it hasn't spread." My heart leaps in my chest. It's over. "But," the Doctor Guy continues, "check in with your urologist next week. I'm sure he's going to want to follow up with you."

Sure, sure, whatever. I. Am. Healed! *Hallelujah!* I hear a chorus of angels playing the mambo. I want to dance with them but my scrotal support is simply too constricting.

A nurse pulls out my IV and wheels me to the hospital exit. My wife pulls up in the car, and I feel like a woman having just been released from childbirth. Except I have no baby.

I have no baby.

And my balls are . . . completely gone . . . every chance of children I have rests on the shoulders of others.

Jade honks the horn, and I saunter over to the car and crawl into the passenger seat. She hands me the manila folder and says, "One last surprise." I open the file and find three digital photos that have been printed out on high gloss paper, each one more gruesome than the last.

She says, "I figured that little bastard has given you so many problems in the last month you'd at least want to see his face."

Inside are three pictures of my bloody testicle sitting on a blue rag with a small gray tumor stuck to its side. We go home, frame one, and put it on a shelf in our living room.

Jade says, "We made it. We survived cancer."

CHAPTER 14
THE BLACK TENDRILS

Cancer surgery is not like having your tonsils or your appendix or your pancreas removed. Cancer is not something you can point your finger at and say, "It is here and this is the problem and this is the solution and now you can go home." Cancer is more like, "It's here-ish, and if we do *this* it should hopefully fix most of the problem, but we really won't know until we do it. Let's just eat the cow one bite at a time, shall we?"

So, after my surgery wherein I was miraculously cured thanks to the advancements of modern medicine, my urologist, Dr. Honda, asked for a follow-up visit to see how I was doing and to see my scar and to do some blood work and the process goes on and on, and like a leaf in a river stream, I'm stuck in it, and I just float along, going wherever the current points, and right now the current has pointed me to a chair behind an oak desk. On the other side of the desk sits Dr. Honda, a man who I've come to love in a very strange way, having played such a large part in saving my life. I feel very close to him, and I find his presence comforting. It is this man who has completely eradicated the cancer from my body. It is this man who has removed the looming venomous poison from my person. And it's this man who is now telling me that the cancer is still there. That it isn't gone. That they didn't get it all. That it has spread to my lymph nodes. And it's me staring at this man and saying, "A lynf-what? And how many do I have? And what does that mean?" and I feel like it's one of those days where everything keeps going wrong, where you can't find your shoes and then you break your laces and then your car is out of gas and then you find out your cancer is back.

More images of sick kids with black sunken eyes pass through my mind, images of cardboard cutouts at cash registers in cheap restaurants. "Donate a quarter to Alex, and you could save him from leukemia." Only instead of Alex, it's me. And there are no quarters. Because some bastard probably stole them. Because that's the kind of luck I'm having.

"How many lymph nodes? Well, the human body has about 700." I mouth the number silently to myself and try to compare that to my one single testicle. Listen, I'm no math whiz but I know that 700 problems is worse than one.

Dr. Honda says, "The lymph nodes, they, they move things around. They connect your body. They're—the easiest way to explain it is—they're a transit system. Like a subway."

And I say, "And can cancer ride on this subway?" and he adjusts his glasses but never breaks eye contact with me. He says, "Yes, it can."

Jade squeezes my hand with the ferocity of a vice grip and my fingers are just wet noodles, both my arms dangling limply at my sides, my head

100

cocked one way, and just who does this guy think he is, telling me I have cancer when I just had my poisonous tumor removed—removed with the cancer? I traded my nut for safety and health, and *I paid the price!* But, like all things with cancer, it doesn't care about you. Because it is you. Slowly eating itself like the snake with its own ass in its mouth. Sorry, buddy. Bottoms up. The Black Tendrils stretch through my body, and I feel their presence inside me, throbbing, somewhere, everywhere, poison.

I say, "What do we do? How do we . . . stop it . . . from spreading?" and he says, "I'd like to remove them," and I say, "Them? Them what? Them t he cancers?" and he says, "No, the lymph nodes. I want to remove them. We would open you from your collar bone to your groin and pull them each out individually," and I say, "But . . . there are 700. Don't I . . . need them?" and he says, "You will have a weakened immune system, yes."

" . . . And a pretty sweet scar," I mumble.

He tells me he's scheduling us an appointment with an oncologist, and I say, "Is that someone who's on call all the time?" and my wife let's out one of those weird pig noises people make when they're crying really, really hard but then something makes them laugh. She says, "It's not funny," and I say, "I know. This is serious," and she says, "No. Your joke. It's not funny. It's really, really, bad."

CHAPTER 15
. . . AND I'M DROWNING
SLOWLY

It's pretty difficult for my wife and I to find common ground in terms of musical taste. At the top of this list that is only two bands long is Ben Folds Five, a group that gained popularity in the '90s for their song "Brick." *She's a brick and I'm drowning slow-ly / She's a brick and I'm* something something. That's the song you would know. Even if you don't know the band, that's a song you've heard.

So, as you do when a band you like comes to town, you begrudgingly purchase well over-priced tickets, and you wait. The show was to be celebratory. We heard about it while we were still in the throes of chaos with the testicular cancer—back at the very beginning—and thought to ourselves, "This will be a treat. This will be our special gift for coming out the other side. Everyone should have a special gift for losing their only remaining testicle."

But then, like a certain pesky cat in a catchy nursery rhyme, the cancer came back the very next day. Thought he was a goner, but the cancer came back.

Now everything had a thundercloud looming over it. I was looking at everything through shit-colored glasses. I still ate food, but I did it with cancer. I still read books, but I did it with cancer. I still masturbated, but I did it with cancer watching me, always on my mind, always ruining the mood I was trying to set in the bathroom with all the candles and incense and whale music. I still went to work, but I did it with cancer.

My boss walks in the room and asks me something about zombies, and I skip the conversation and say, "I still have cancer," and he sits down and is looking at me like I'm the handicapped puppy again and he says, "That's . . . . OK . . . . So . . . " and I say, "I'm seeing an oncologist in a week or so. They're, I don't know. They're talking about chemotherapy," and he sucks in air really quickly through his teeth and clicks his pen a couple times and says, *Really?* like maybe I misheard them.

I say, "Yes," and he's very accommodating, but I suspect that it might be because, as a manager, he's never been in this position before. I tell him, "I plan to keep working or whatever, so, I mean, I'll do whatever I can. I'm not quitting my job—I'm just . . . I don't know. I might need to take off for doctor's appointments sometimes but I can make up the lost time on nights or weekends and I'm OK with that," and he says, "Yeah, yeah, yeah, OK. Good. Yes, whatever you need. Whatever you need, you just do it and your job is here and we'll work with you however you need and we'll just take it one day at a time," and then silence.

And then he says, "Sucks."

And then he leaves.

And then it's the day of the Ben Folds Five concert, and I sort of am not feeling like going out to a concert because everything depresses me. The truth is, I really wish I just had a big fat joint right now, some weed to just pack and pack and pack into the biggest bowl I can find, but there's nothing in my house and there hasn't been since I ran out right after Las Vegas. Ever since this cancer thing started, I've become hyper aware of my health and my body and I'm just trying to be as clean as possible. But still. It would be nice. Maybe instead of going out we could just lie on the couch . . . .

No.

I sit up quickly and say, "Let's go," and my wife says, "Are you sure? We really—we really don't have to. Let's not go if it's just for me—I'd rather—I don't know. We can just lie on the couch. We can even shut the lights off. We can even shut our eyes. We can just be depressed," and I consider her offer but then say, "No. It can't win," and that's a very obvious and heroic movie line thing to say but it feels very true. It was destroying me, inside and out, and I was letting it take something as wonderful as my love of music away. I think there is nothing quite like a live performance in all of the world and I was *allowing* cancer to rob me of it.

I slam the keys into the ignition, and I drive at top speeds across Los Angeles, and I say to hell with it, and I park in valet and I drop the extra dough because *tonight is my special gift. It is mine and it doesn't belong to Cancer.* I am going to stand at the front of the crowd. I'm going to push my way to the very front, and I'm going to scream every lyric I know and probably just go, "Daahh-gaah-hmm," to the parts I don't, but I'm going to do it with the veracity of a real live person who isn't dying, except . . . when we go into the theater we realize that it's not that kind of concert. We realize this venue only supports stadium seating. And we realize that we're in the balcony. In the back row. Against the wall. This is nosebleed. This is air-traffic control.

Ben is a little speck on the stage, and I can sort of make out his piano, and we're already pretty late since we were debating the show to begin with, and I have to wonder if we've missed some of our favorite songs. Another fantastic stroke of luck; another feather in the hat; another golden egg.

Sitting in the small chair, I try to cross my legs and feel the stitches in my abdomen stretch and pull, and I get comfortable again and this concert is *so boring.* He's just . . . playing the piano and . . . I mean, I guess that's what he does, that's what I *paid for* technically but . . . . . I sit back and shut my eyes and try to imagine I'm just listening to the CD while I lie on my couch at home.

While I'm trying to find my Zen place, a knee bumps mine, and I open my eyes to find some girl, probably about my age, is trying to sit down in the

106

cramped quarters to my right. She's got on a black mini-skirt and a white tank top and a tattoo of both a snake and an eagle on her arm, but she doesn't look like the type of girl who should have either a snake or an eagle tattooed on her arm. Her black hair bobs under her chin, and she's really made up to be out on some hot date. I look past her and see that some dude—I mean, that is really the best way to describe this guy—is tagging along behind her, bumping into everyone in the row, trying to get to his seat. He doesn't apologize or say excuse me, he's just straight from the trailer court to the concert, and he's really big like he used to work out but not so much anymore. Like he used to love the gym but now he loves pot.

They both sit down next to me, and I sigh and smile and try to be polite, and she asks me, "Are we late?" and I look at the stage and see the band performing on it and say, "Uh . . . I think so," and she laughs and says, "*Whatev!* You mind if I smoke?" and I say, "I . . . don't care," and she pulls out this joint and just lights it up, right there. Sitting inside a theater, in a chair, surrounded by people who are not smoking or drinking and are sort of just fuds, she lights up and starts getting high. She passes the joint to her boyfriend, and the smell is so good. I just close my eyes and imagine lying on my couch, listening to the Ben Folds Five CD and smoking a joint. Boy, that would just feel great right now. I've got a friend that used to say, "Weed makes a good thing great and a bad thing . . . not so bad!" and then he would inhale and stare at me with eyes on fire and give me that stupid cheese-out grin and cough.

Jade leans over and says, "Are those people . . . smoking *weed* . . . in *here*?" and I laugh and I say, "Yeah, I guess," and it really is pretty funny. The theater we're in seems pretty hobnobby and the crowd seems very straight-laced and sort of on the older side and very subdued and this girl and her dude-guy are just getting baked. They are experiencing total freedom.

Ben finishes another song just as The Girl and The Dude finish their joint. I watch her out of the corner of my eye—she is infinitely more entertaining than the show—as she delicately crushes the end out between two wet fingers and then stomps on the cherry, crushing it into the glossy cement floor. She opens a little coin purse, pulls out a baggie and places the roach inside, closes the baggie, closes the coin purse, closes her *purse majora* and sits back and starts to sort of dance in her chair, feeling the groove, I suppose, and I wish I were feeling the groove, as well.

Ben is doing his best. He's playing the piano with his elbows, and he's banging on the keys with his fists, and he's actually reaching *inside* the piano and is just pulling on the strings in there and, probably if I were closer to the stage and had less on my mind, this would be pretty cool.

The Girl suddenly turns to me and leans in and sort of whisper-shouts in my ear, "Oh, hey! I'm so sorry! I'm so selfish! I didn't give you any! Do you wanna smoke?" and I don't even hesitate. My heart doesn't beat twice before I answer. I don't let that logical part of my brain speak. I don't think about health or clean eating. I just think about stress and release and celebration and just blurt out, "Yes. Yes. Please."

Total freedom.

She pulls out her purse, and she pulls out a second baggie that's packed to the gills with weed and she pulls out some zigzags and begins to roll a brand-new joint, and I just keep thinking about how the cannabis community is filled with some of the most generous people I have ever met.

Jade leans over and asks, "What did she say?" and I say, "She asked me if I wanted to get high," and Jade says, "Oh," assuming that the conversation ended there.

The Girl dumps a row of smelly grass onto the paper and then another row and sort of mashes it down and then sprinkles a bit on top of that just for good measure. *This chick is going to get us baked*, I think to myself as she lights it herself and then hands it to me.

I lean in and, not sure exactly what the proper etiquette for a stranger handing you free drugs at a concert is, I just whisper-shout, "Thank you!" and then I put the joint to my lips and pull and inhale and out of the corner of my eye Jade is just *staring at me*, and I turn to her and she says, "*What is this?*" and I say, "I'm getting fucking high tonight, baby," and I hand her the joint and she stares at it, and I know exactly what she's thinking. She's thinking, *Fuck it. Let's make lemonade!* She pinches the joint and takes a hit and shrugs and passes it back to me, and I try to pass it back to the owner, the four of us sharing, and The Girl leans into me and says, "No, no. That's yours!" and I'm looking at this Cheech and Chong sized white paper bratwurst in my hand and I'm like, "You got it."

Ben is playing beautifully and his stage performance is extravagant and his showmanship and the light show—the light show!—everything about this show is fantastic, down to the beautiful, blessed seats that are so *high.* Yellow skulls, stretched and distorted, are being projected onto the billowing curtains, eternally being pulled up, up, up, onto, into the ceiling. White spotlights pan the audience, and lasers of various colors and sizes blast sharp beams out, penetrating and cutting through the darkness. The music builds and builds and builds and, even though I'm staring at skulls floating in front of my eyes, I'm not thinking of death and I'm not thinking of dying and I'm certainly not thinking of cancer. Everything is just good and great and wonderful!

I pull the joint up to my lips, and Ben slams his fists into the keys, making jarring notes that are fitting for the cacophonistic end of the song, and I start thinking about aliens watching us—everyone sitting in the dark, staring at a single person on a stage, all of us chanting the same words in perfect rhythm like a prayer. I can't get over this thought, this Outside Earth Perspective I've got going on, and I think I might be projecting some weird things so I try to just focus back on the music as it begins to crescendo. I inhale and feel myself get lifted a little higher. As I begin to slowly blow the smoke out in one great big billowing cloud of silver fog, Ben hits the keys with both hands as hard as he can and Every. Single. Light in the theater flares on in time to the music and I have to notice that I am just *surrounded* by a purple haze and I am the only one in the place encircled by this mist and it's so tangible and palpable that an image of Pig Pen from *Charlie Brown* actually pops into my head.

A man in front of me in a brown suit, short black hair flattened and gelled against his head, turns around and gives me the stank eye and, yes, I am busted. There's no denying this. I am *that guy* right now. His wife or girlfriend or whoever she is, turns around, along with several other members of their party, and I just smile because there's nothing else I can do.

The arena goes dark again, and I'm grateful because I was feeling pretty naked and exposed. The Girl and The Dude next to me stand up and exit the way they came, taking all of their belongings with them right in the middle of one of the songs, and I wonder just what sort of adventures they're going to get into tonight when, suddenly, they reach the main aisle and, instead of exiting the theater, the two of them just begin to dance. Crazy Person Dancing.

Stripper dancing. Grinding and shaking, arms above head, ecstasy induced, hallucinogenic, mind-fry dancing.

Total Freedom.

Total Freedom that is horrifying me right now because the consequences of my decisions suddenly seem very real and paralyzing. I have just taken *drugs* from a *stranger* at a *rock concert*.

I stare at The Girl and The Dude and just keep thinking, *What did I just smoke? What did I just smoke? What was in the weed? What else was in the weed? Do I feel all messed up? Am I high? Am I just weed high or am I, like, going to start freaking out pretty soon?*

I've never done anything "beyond" marijuana and so I am on the edge of my seat, trying to hyper analyze and over analyze and scrutinize every feeling I'm experiencing and *SHIT! What if those people in front of me are cops?! What am I doing smoking weed in a public place around a bunch of people in suits? What kind of a dipshit am I? This wasn't very responsible! SHIT! That girl is dancing on the floor! She's on her knees dancing and she doesn't know what she's doing or where she's at and I bet she's hallucinating and pretty soon* I'm *going to be hallucinating and* I'm *going to be dancing in the aisle,* and so I lean over to Jade and go, "I don't know what I just smoked. What are they doing?" and Jade shrugs and says, "I only took a couple hits. Did you . .

. " and then she realizes that the entire submarine sandwich joint has been consumed by me because I have no stop button and just keep smoking and smoking until it's gone.

I squeeze the armrests of the chair and try to will myself to relax.

The Girl and The Dude disappear and the concert is over and Jade and I stand up and rush out of the theater. On the sidewalk there is a black man in a hospital gown with a handmade sign asking for money. I walk past him and pretend he doesn't exist. The two of us walk into a Denny's because it's 1 o'clock ante meridiem and we're coming down and have the munchies. We both order pancakes, and as I'm watching the Hospital-Gowned Homeless Man out the window, I see two cops walk past him and then I have the exact same thought anyone who's ever been high and has seen cops thinks, which is, *Crap! Cops!*

Now I give *them* the stank eye, even though they can't see me, and try to will them to pass the building. But they don't. They enter the restaurant, and I'm sure that someone at the theater has given them my description and they're looking for me and so I just focus on my pancakes. *Fork in left hand and knife in right hand and just—wait—you're right handed, switch the fork and knife—no, wait, it was right—you had it right—just cut slow—what . . . is this how a human cuts pancakes? Do I look like a human?*"

113

We finish our dinner-breakfast, walk back to our car, and just as we open our doors, we hear a woman scream. We look over the balcony of the parking garage and see Ben or Ben Folds or Ben-Whatever-His-Last-Name-Is has emerged from the venue and twenty-some 20-somethings all shake pieces of paper and digital cameras and cell phones at him, and he slowly approaches each person, individually. I clear my throat and bark, "*HEY*!" and everyone suddenly stops what they're doing and looks toward me, including Ben. I shout, "Great show!" and he waves.

Jade and I get back in the car, drive home, and lie on the couch. She puts his CD on, and I think about the possibility of a medicinal marijuana card.

PART 3

"It's the end of the world as we know it, and I feel . . . ."
-R.E.M.

CHAPTER 16
AGGRESSIVE ACCELERATION

Dr. Odegaard, the GP who had made my very first "there is definitely a lump" diagnosis some 30 days ago and had recommended me to Dr. Honda, my urologist, has now recommended an oncologist for me to meet with at White Memorial Hospital in downtown Los Angeles.

My wife and I enter the hospital and find that the main lobby is under construction and is being poorly partitioned. Dust and specks of insulation and dirt and cement and broken tile lie about and float in the air. It's less hospital and more third-world-country-post-war-zone chic. I ask the receptionist where I should be, and she directs me to an elevator that looks as though it were designed and installed at the turn of the century and hasn't had a maintenance check since. Upon exiting my floor I find red (blood/rust/chemical/vomit/paint??) stains on the carpet and water stains on the ceiling.

All hospitals are not created equal.

I enter the waiting room, and the very first thing I notice is that there are patients *everywhere*; all the chairs packed, people standing and sitting on the floor, nearly stepping on one another, two and three deep and I just keep thinking, "There are so many. So many sick people. There aren't enough doctors here."

And while I focus on this weird ratio of patients to professionals, I wait . . . and wait . . . and wait . . . .

An hour past my appointment time, I approach the window and ask for an ETA on my "reservation" and they tell me that they're running about 90 minutes behind schedule. I ask if a doctor got sick and the receptionist says, "No," and I ask, "Is this pretty standard?" and she sort of gives me a shy I'm-not-supposed-to-say-this type smile and it's enough of an answer for me. I sit back in my chair and mumble angrily to myself and wish there were some sort of air freshener in this room because it's starting to smell like body sweat.

Thirty minutes later, they call my name—"Mr. Brootbagk"—and lead me like a lamb to the slaughter (you know the feeling), and once I get into the doctor's exam room I wait more and more *and more*, and it's not the kind of waiting that one expects in a doctor's office. It is the endless abyss of waiting where time stretches on indefinitely and seconds become hours and you wonder if the doctor is just enjoying a ham sandwich in the break room.

The door finally opens and someone enters. A young man. A doctor. He sits down and calls me the wrong name, I correct him, at which point he realizes he's in the incorrect room. Leaves. We wait. A second doctor enters. Asks me two questions, and gets my name right. Excuses himself. We wait. We wait. We wait. A third doctor enters. He sits down and asks me what my name is and what I'm doing here. He has no folder, no information on us or my surgery or background. He's just winging it off the cuff, I guess. He exits. He returns with our folder.

The doctor tells me that I have stage 2 cancer. He tells me they biopsied my testicle (put it in a blender and looked at the goop under a microscope). He tells me that there are two different kinds of cancer; there is *nonseminoma* and there is just plain old *seminoma* and that I have the first. I take a deep breath, relieved, because clearly, "non" is always better. He sighs and says, "Nonseminoma is actually the more aggressive of the two," and now, every comedic deflection I have is being ground out of me and my lip begins to quiver and I still don't understand why this is happening. He tells me, "Nonseminoma breaks down into four categories and you also have the most aggressive of the four."

I say, "The most aggressive of the most aggressive . . . " and he says, "Yes," and my hand has turned purple and then white from Jade squeezing it and I look over and see that she has mascara and tears streaming down her cheeks and her eyes are red and her face is puffy and I feel like I'm going to pass out but manage to say, "So . . . what . . . does that . . . mean?" And I say this because . . . what else do you say? How else do you respond? Someone tells you that you have some of the most aggressive cancer on Earth and—

The doctor says, "I'd like to admit you today, right now. I'd like you to start chemotherapy," and my breath catches in my throat because now I am a Cancer Patient. More visions of ghostly bald kids with hollow eyes shoot through my brain and images of me hiding somewhere in the crowd with my IV, pulling it sadly behind me. I ask the doctor, "But . . . my job. I work tomorr—" and before I'm even done with my sentence he's shaking his head. "No. You're not. You won't work again until this is over," and I say, "But I can work. I can make it work—they're cool with my schedule," and he says, "No. You won't work. You won't read. You won't watch TV. I just want to be very transparent with you about this—I've seen this take men in the military down to . . . nothing," and I just keep thinking, "Why is he telling me this? Why is he saying these things?" and me, grabbing at straws, trying to make ends meet, throwing myself at any possible outcome that doesn't involve chemotherapy, say, "Dr. Honda—he says he wants to pull out my lymph nodes! Cut me open from gullet to groin and pluck pluck pluck! We can just do that!" because, in my head, surgery is not as *serious* as chemotherapy. Surgery is manageable and understandable and considerably more familiar ground but the doctor says, "No. It's . . . . That's not possible. The cancer is too aggressive and it's moving fast. We have to just get you into chemotherapy as soon as possible and try to kill it—" (me) "—that way. It's our best shot. Surgery will just delay it and, ultimately, you'll still have to undergo chemo *just to make sure.*"

My wife is still crying and he says, "I'll get the paperwork," and I say, "No," and the doctor says,

120

"What's that now?" and I say, "No. We're not checking in here."

And we rise up and we leave, pushing blindly through walls and walls and walls made of patients on standby.

In the car, we call Dr. Honda, our urologist who had suggested pulling out my lymph nodes, and we tell him about our experience at White Memorial. I tell him about the floors and the ceiling and the dust and the dirt and the waiting and the missing files and the three doctors and *all the people just standing there* and I say, "I can't do that. I can't leave my life in the hands of those people. I just . . . . If I have to do chemotherapy, fine, I have to do it *but you make sure I have to do it* and please, please, please, just put me somewhere else. I don't *trust* them."

We hang up the phone and it immediately rings with an unrecognized number. Curiosity wins out and my wife clicks it open while I drive. "Hello?" she says.

It's the doctor from White Memorial.

"Please," he says, "I can't stress this enough. You *must* check in somewhere today. You *must* begin treatment today. Your disease is so aggressive—" (There's that word again, like a mad dog or a cage fighter or an acid: *aggressive.*) "—it's not something to mess around with. Just . . . please." And then, "Why don't you come back? *I* can be your oncologist." At first he sounded like he was genuinely pleading my case and then it sounded like he was freshly employed, and needed the experience under his belt and so my wife tells him, in the politest way possible, that his hospital reminded us of any number of post-apocalyptic movies.

There's a pause on the phone and the doctor speaks again, softer. He says, "I understand. Fine. But please, listen to me. *Listen*. Don't mess around with this. I don't care where you go, just . . . go. Go somewhere. Go there now and check in," and my wife says, "Thank you," and hangs up and neither of us says anything but we both recognize something so desperate in his voice that we each have to wonder just what it is we're dealing with here.

We know it's bad but . . . how bad? How *aggressive*?
Several days later, my wife and I are finally sitting in front of Dr. Honda and, yes, I know the last doctor said we needed to check in ASAP, but the truth is, there are channels one must go through and sometimes those channels are clogged by other patients that are not you and you must simply . . . wait.

And that's Cancer: waiting. Waiting in doctor's offices, waiting in exam rooms, waiting in waiting rooms slowly, waiting, dying, healing hopefully, but dying and fearing and waiting.

"Cancer markers," Dr. Honda says and all I can picture is children with thick black markers coloring the walls of a classroom in living venom slime, the dark goo dripping down and running everywhere, growing and attaching to anything with DNA.

"Cancer markers are in your blood. They let us know how much cancer you have. A normal, healthy, cancer-free person would have zero." I say, "OK," because the math seems to make sense. He tells me that previous to my surgery they did a blood test and my cancer markers were at 32 and I say, "*What*?! Thirty-two out of what?! Is that high?!" And he says, "Higher than it should be. Mine is zero," and I shrug because this, too, is sound logic.

He tells me that two days after surgery, my numbers hit 619 and my jaw drops to the floor and my teeth fall out and the doctor says, "Today you hit 900," and now my breathing is shallow and my tongue is dry and everything is blurry and I don't know if I'm crying or if my eyeballs are just dry or if I'm getting faint, but I do the quick math and realize that I now have roughly 30 times the amount of cancer I had a couple days ago when I still had a *bawl*. The doctor at the Ghetto Hospital's voice suddenly rings through my head, and I hear all his desperation with new ears.

I hear that word.

Aggressive.

123

Dr. Honda says, "We need to check you in somewhere," and, making a personal suggestion, he says a good friend of his is an oncologist at Arcadia Methodist. He says it'll be a far drive but— And we don't let him finish the thought. We love him so much that anything he says is Gospel. If he likes the doctor, we like the doctor. We take his word for it and make a bee-line for the place, site unseen.

An hour later, in the parking lot of the hospital, my wife snaps a photo of me standing in front of the monolithic building – a soft, four-story cube. I'm staring directly into the camera with the fullest beard I can grow, a large smile and a full, confident face. It's the last time I'll see that expression for some time. I'm sporting aviator sunglasses, hair, and hope but I'll slowly lose all three of them before long.

WARNING: Please keep your arms and legs inside the vehicle at all times. This trip is about to get bumpy.

***   ***   ***   ***   ***

We walk through the doors and immediately I see the clean, white, sterile, horrible hospital. Even the best hospitals are horrible and hideous and terrible. Even the cleanest and purest and friendliest are hateful places, filled with the sick and the dead and dying. The smell of cleaning supplies masking the stench of vomit hits my nose. The smell of rubbing alcohol and latex and linen mixes with powdered mashed potatoes and powdered scrambled eggs and powdered milk. All roads have led to here. This is the trajectory my entire life has been on, like a rocket aimed at the moon. Houston, we have contact.

I know that I have a long fight in front of me and, although I'm happy to be getting started, I do wish I were instead at home or at work or, really, anywhere. But instead I'm here, in this elevator . . . and now in this hallway . . . and now in this room that will be my home for the next eight days.

I undress, put on the gown, and set my personal belongings on a small shelf. On a table next to the bed, I place a novel I won't open; my iPod, which I will barely turn on; and my journal, which has served as the skeleton and fact checker for this book; journals that I'm eternally thankful for because my brain is about to turn into something slightly softer than Jell-O, something slightly less formless than a raw egg. This is your brain—this is your brain on chemo.

The nurse enters with the IV and my knees lock and my heart speeds up and my forehead starts to sweat and she tells me to lie down. I don't bother fighting it but I tell her how afraid I am and every time, every needle, it never gets easier, it just gets worse and worse and worse. My wife holds my hand and rubs the back of my palms with her thumb and my toes wiggle and I feel the metallic stick slide into my arm and fish around and I'm not breathing and then it's done and she says I can release my fist. She applies some tape and tells me to relax and says that she'll be back in a little bit and now it begins.

I look at the IV pole to my left and I am One of Them. I am a Cancer Patient.

My wife turns on a reality TV show and I try to write in my journal while not upsetting my IV in any fashion, so afraid that it's going to get caught on something and yank out. The TV goes to commercial break just as a man enters the room and tells me they want to do a CAT scan on me and at this point I'm just a sack of potatoes, their puppet, to push around and wheel back and forth and poke and prod and maneuver in any way they see fit, so I say, "OK," and my wife keeps watching a show where a family has eighteen kids and I can't have any.

The giant Mechanical Donut is down in the basement of the hospital and the room is run by two guys who look like they drink lots of beer while consuming pharmaceuticals that they steal from work. They both have tattoos on their arms and long hair, and honestly, it's kind of nice to talk to two people who aren't "doctors" or "nurses" or "hospital staff" but just "dudes." I ask them how long they've been working here and what they want to be doing long term and they ask me what I've got and what I'm doing and they're pretty impressed with my weird story about cancer and they tell me about how they once gave David Hasselhoff a CAT scan.

The bed shifts and moves and pulls me into the donut and the same female robot from the first hospital (different donut) says, "Hold. Your. Breath." I do and I turn my head to the left, trying to relax. On the wall is a motivational poster with a photo of a stream and the caption: IN THE BATTLE BETWEEN WATER AND THE ROCK, THE WATER WILL ALWAYS WIN. NOT BECAUSE OF STRENGTH, BUT BECAUSE OF PERSISTENCE. I look back at the ceiling and try to decide if I find this cheesy or poignant or both. The stoner guy says, "Here comes the dye," and I feel like I just pissed my pants.

The David Hasselhoff guy wheels me back to my room and wishes me luck and I still think about him often. I wonder if he's still working next to that Mechanical Donut and I wonder how many times he's told his David Hasselhoff story and I wonder if he's ever met David Hasselhoff again.

My wife asks me if everything went well and I sort of shrug and say, "I think I still have cancer but . . . the machine didn't blow up whilst I was inside of it, if that's what you're asking," and she says, "Good," and then turns her attention back to the TV, where a sweaty woman is giving birth and screaming.

I pick up my cell phone, an old Motorola Razor (you know it's badass because it's named after a blade) and call my mom. She says, "Hi, sweetie! How is your *daaaay*!?" and again, I just want to reiterate that I wasn't expecting this. I wasn't planning on sleeping in a hospital tonight. It wasn't marked on my calendar. So you can see the loaded question here. "Well, uh . . . " I say, "I'm doing good. Sort of. I'm, uh, my cancer is back," and there's silence on the phone and then quiet crying. I say, "I'm in the hospital right now," and panic is setting in with her, *Are you OK? What's wrong?*" and I say, "I'm, uh, I'm getting chemotherapy," and there's more quiet crying and I hear my dad in the background ask what's wrong and he takes the phone and he says, "Hello?" and I say, "It's me," and he says, "Oh. What's wrong?" and I say, "Nothing's *wrong*, I mean . . . yeah. I'm in the hospital. I'm getting chemotherapy. My cancer is back—or—it never left, I guess. They didn't get it all. I'll be here for a while— I'll be here for a week. About eight days," and my dad says, "We're coming out."

A few hours later an old man enters my room pushing a cart that smells like cafeteria food. He places a tray on my bedside table and says, *"Bon appetit!"* and then vanishes. Because I haven't eaten since previous to my appointment with Dr. Honda, my stomach is grumbling and I don't care what's under that plate cover, it's going in mouth and down my throat. I lift up the warm lid and there is absolutely no amount of money that would sway me into placing that food on my tongue. The menu would probably call it "meatloaf" but I would call it "gunk at back of fridge mashed into patty formation." The fact that it's swimming in powdered gravy doesn't bother me so much as the fact that the powdered gravy is the consistency of snot. I ask Jade if she wants any and she says, "Uh, no, thank you," and then I say, "I dare you to take a bite of this meatloaf," and she says, "No," and I say, "No, seriously. What would it take for you to take a bite of this meatloaf?" and she says, "A one-hour back rub," and I say, "OK. Fine," because I really want to see her gag. She looks at the plate and then, reconsidering, "I can't do it."

I put the lid back on the tray and scoot the entire table toward the door where the smell is least offensive while my wife leaves to purchase us Panda Express.

She's gone for about forty-five minutes while I just sit in the room, alone, reflecting, and I will soon find out that this is one of the biggest problems with cancer. When you can't do anything, all you can do is dwell on yourself, your problem, your condition.

It's not so bad right now and my attitude is pretty good and I'm certain it's just going to be like getting the flu and that doctor didn't know what he was talking about when he said that it would *shut me down*. I'm not a robot.

People walk by in the hallway and there is a general background noise happening out there—talking and footsteps and intercoms and beeping. And so I get up and shut the door and turn on the TV but can't find anything to watch so I put in my earphones and think of Ben (Folds) and wonder what he's doing right now—some guy somewhere that has no idea where I am, what I'm doing. He's playing a show, punching his piano, and signing autographs and here I am, remembering him while I drown out everything else.

I open my eyes and Jade is standing in the room, staring at me, a big white bag of fast food in her hands. She says, "Dinner bell," and I sit up while she sits at the foot of the bed. She pulls over the coffee table, which is now empty—I assume someone came in and took the "food" while my eyes were closed—and we eat dinner, we watch TV, we talk, and we wonder when The Chemotherapy will begin.

Eight o'clock rolls around and still no drugs so I hit my buzzer and a nurse enters who has a very sweet face and I ask her when I'll be starting my "thing" and she tells me, "Tomorrow, in the morning," and I smile and nod my head and am not sure if this is good news or bad news or indifferent news. The nurse leaves and Jade snuggles up next to me. There is a cot in the room but we don't use it. That night the two of us just crush our bodies together in a platonic, nonsexual, but still really desperately needy way and sleep in very broken segments, two kids that are stupid and lost and scared.

*** *** *** *** ***

In the morning, the old man serves us "eggs" and "bacon" and "toast" but the only thing either of us consumes is the "fruit." Neither of us are big breakfast eaters nor fans of food that tastes like someone's vinegar-soaked jock strap.

There's another reality show on TV and I think this one might be about wedding disasters and the victims therein. Sigh, tragedy. My wife is locked on, saying, "What! Shut . . . *up* . . . What?" and then the nurse who gave me my IV yesterday is back but she's wearing a full hazmat suit over her regular nurse get-up and she has on a face mask and gloves and she carries a dark bag that's covered in plastic.

I ask, "What is . . . that?" but I already know the answer. She says, "This is bleomycin; it's the first of four medicines you'll be receiving today."

Medicine. Boy, we're really throwing that word around, aren't we? I imagine that in the future, people will say, "Can you believe they used to give patients chemo??? They poisoned them to cure them—how savage! Luckily, the scientists have found the cure for cancer in oil. *Too bad we used it all driving our SUVs with only one person in the car and now the polar bears are all dead because of global warming! Hip-hip-hooray! The future really is a brighter place. But only because the atmosphere has finally dissolved and the sun is now shining directly onto our reddened, burnt skin! Yay for technology! Yay!*

I unconsciously slide away from the IV pole, trying to put distance between us and I say, "Why is it in two bags?" and the nurse says, "So if it leaks it doesn't spill," and I say, "And why are you dressed like that?" and she says, "So in case it spills it doesn't get on my skin," and I say, "And where is that going?" and she says, "Into your IV," and I swallow hard.

She hangs the bag upside down and allows gravity to do what it does best. She plugs a tube into one of my ports and turns a small dial with her thumb. I watch the liquid drip-drip-drop from the bag and race toward my arm and I hold my breath. Here it comes. Here it is. And I say, in a strained voice, "Will this hurt?" and the nurse says, "No," but I don't believe her. The clear liquid enters my body and she's right. I don't feel anything.

Drip-drip-drip.

She tells me she'll be back in about two hours and then leaves. Jade turns from the TV and sits down next to me on the bed and we both watch each little drop race down into my body and my wife says, "Each drop is you getting better. We'll be OK."

Drip-drip-drip.

CHAPTER 17
NODULES

I open my eyes and immediately notice two things: The first is that the sun is trying to peek through my blinds, scooping its rays around the edge of the window. The second is that I feel incredibly hung over and the sensation seems to just be amplifying by the second. I take several deep breaths and fumble around in the gray light, looking for a cup of water while trying not to wake my wife.

I manage to kick my feet off the side of the bed and take three big gulps from a cup filled with something that's the same temperature as horse spit. My stomach churns and rolls and I gag and the water rises up my esophagus and into my mouth. I hop off the bed, pursing my lips and waddle into the cramped bathroom, pulling my IV (mine, mine, mine) behind me. I bend over and open my mouth and the three gulps fall gracefully into the toilet like Olympians at the high dive. Ker-*splash*.

I gag, gag, gag again but nothing comes up. I sit down on the floor and hear Jade in the other room shift around, "Are you OK?"

"I'm just . . . sick."

A nurse enters and asks if everything is OK and I tell him that I puked and he tells me that it's a side effect. I thank him and expect him to leave but instead he takes my blood and I wonder if they're going to do another cancer marker test and if those numbers are going to be lower than 900.

Jade turns on the television and the show with the million kids is on again so I just turn my head and stare at the *drip-drip-drip* and try to imagine my numbers dropping, *900-899-898*, even though I know there's no possible way it could be decreasing so rapidly.

By lunch the nausea has increased so much that I consider just making camp in the bathroom. I keep munching on ice chips but my wife continues to suggest that I eat something solid. "Panda Express?" she asks, "In-N-Out?" she asks, "Chipotle?" she asks.

I cover my eyes with my forearm and gag. I tell her she should just go grab some-*gag*-thing for her-*gag*-self. She leaves and a nurse enters and takes my blood and I wonder what those cancer markers look like: numbers floating around in my blood like alphabet soup? The nurse thanks me for some reason and then I flip through the channels and, of course, there's nothing on, so I just find the least offensive show I can and dig in, some episode of *Family Guy,* but it's on the final act so it ends too quickly and then I watch an episode of *Seinfeld* and Jade is back with food and I manage to take a couple bites.

The Hazmat Nurse comes back in and changes my bag to Medicine #2, something called Platinum and I can only picture Madonna. "*One bag down!*" I think and am genuinely happy. "I feel a bit pukey but this isn't so hard!" The Hazmat Nurse exits and a short Asian woman in a yellow shirt and lanyard around her neck enters. "I'm Dr. Yen," she says and offers a tight but friendly smile, adjusting her glasses with her index finger. "I'll be your oncologist, OK?" This is the good friend/specialist to whom Dr. Honda had recommended us. This is the woman who will oversee the ritual. This is our personal witch doctor. She smiles politely and says, "How are you feeling?" and I tell her that I'm a little nauseated and she tells me that it's normal and that she'll order me some anti-nausea medication. I thank her and ask what I should expect and she takes a few steps toward my IV pole, examines the bag and then takes a few steps back. She says, "Here's what we're dealing with. Most people, your regular cancer patient, they're going to get what's called outpatient chemo, OK? There's a clinic, like the one at my office, and they come there and hang out for a couple hours, OK, and they leave and go home and go to work and then come back two weeks later and get another two-hour treatment and so on and so forth, OK, until we've, uh, eradicated the cancer, all right? OK?" and I say, "OK. But that's not what I'm doing," and she says, "No."

She walks around the bed and looks at the Panda Express and says, "Panda Express. Man, I love those egg rolls," and my wife smiles and offers her one, but Dr. Yen shakes her head and says, "No, I try not to eat them. Too greasy." Jade sighs and pops half of it in her mouth while the doctor continues.

"You're going to stay with us for six days and we're going to give you chemotherapy every day, for six hours a day. Six and six. Once it's over, we'll release you back to your home for two weeks and then, *just* when you start feeling better, we're going to bring you back in," and I say, "Uh . . . wow," and she says, "We're going to do this three or four times," and I say, " . . . All right."

She asks me if I have any questions and I say, "A million," and she says, "Shoot," and the first and foremost that's been resting on my brain for the past month is, "Am I going to die?" and with wildly strong confidence she answers, "No. You won't die. Well, I won't say *won't*. I'll say you shouldn't die because there's *always that chance* but your odds are very good. You're young. You're strong," and I say, "OK. Then do what you have to do," and she says, "Listen to me. I'm going to hit you with a Mack truck. I'm going to run you over. I'm going to take you right to the edge . . . and then I'm going to bring you back. You're not going to like me very much," and I just smile and look at the bag and say, "Keep them—" *gag* "—coming."

*** *** *** *** ***

The only thing that's saving me, poison or not, is the constant, *drip-drip-drip* that's running into my arm. The miracle of modern medicine. The blessing of science and technology.

Later that night, my parents show up, having driven straight through from Mitchell, South Dakota,

136

all the way to Los Angeles over night. It's a 1,500-mile trip and they took it in one 22-hour hit.

My mom walks into the room first and throws her purse in a chair and bends down over me and hugs me and just cries. I say, "It's OK, it's OK. I'm just fine," and she says, "You're not fine! You have *cancer! You're getting chemotherapy! You keep telling me you're fine on the phone and it's not a big deal but Theresa* (my sister) *ran into June* (my mother-in-law) *and she says that you're not well at all and that this IS a big deal and that you haven't been completely up front with us about this! John Lowell . . . what . . . how sick are you?*" and I say, "The doctor says I'll probably survive," and my mother wails and says, "*Pro-bab-lee*?!" in all italics like that and holds me tight and it's not until years later when I have children of my own that I'm able to actually imagine a shadow of the pain and fear she must have been experiencing.

She loosens her grip and leans back and I say, "Mother?" and she says, "What?" and I say, "Listen. I just need to tell you . . . that . . . you have . . . mascara running down your face," and she laughs and slaps me and says, "John *Lowell*. Shut *up*. Mas*cara*." She stands up and exits into the bathroom to fix herself up while my dad bends down and gives me one of those Dad Hugs that is sort of in the styling of one-arm-draped-loosely-around-your-neck-side-squeeze things and then quickly stands up and says, "You look good. Down in the parking lot I told your mom that she needed to be ready because you were probably going

137

to look pretty sick, like one of those kids on the quarter collections you see in restaurants but—you look good."

He sits down and says, "They feed you here?" and I say, "Not food," and my mom comes out of the bathroom and says, "Did you guys eat?" and Jade says, "I ate. He's been feeling pretty sick," and I realize that it's already happening. They're starting to talk about me like I'm not here, like I'm just this *thing* that's happening and everyone needs to *take care of.*

The next several days play out in a slow-motion blur of blood withdrawals, bad food, reality shows, chemotherapy bags, good nurses, bad nurses, sleeping, and vomiting. I become intimately acquainted with the toilet as I bow down before the porcelain throne and give my tithe.

My parents come and go—they're staying at our house while they're in town—and Jade, working a part-time job, stays the night with me if she doesn't have to work in the morning. The second and third night she sleeps on the cot because, as romantic and harlequin as it is for two young lovers to share a single hospital bed, it is actually extremely uncomfortable and nearly impossible to sleep while your partner continues to shudder with dry—*gag*—heaves.

Nurses periodically bring me nausea medication but it's never quick enough to stop the sickness or strong enough to fight it back. They try pills and they try intravenous injections and it seems to take the edge off but not enough to actually stop it from cutting.

On November 26, while my wife is outside the hospital smoking a cigarette (I won't even get into the irony of it), an older gentleman sporting a plaid button-up and thick glasses enters my room and introduces himself as Dr. Sharpe, a partner to Dr. Yen. He tells me that she's busy at their office today but he wanted to come by to quickly speak with me.

I say, "Nice to meet you," and he pulls up a chair and says, "Likewise," although there is no smile in his voice. It's just a word rolling off a tongue, a guttural noise that has some human meaning.

He opens a manila folder, pulls the glasses from his face, and holds them halfway between himself and the paper. "The reports of your CAT scan are back and it says here that you have several nodules on your lungs."

Silence.
"Nodules? What is that? What is—"

"Sorry. Tumors."

"Tumors? On my lungs?" and there are so, so many thoughts flying through my head at this one moment but the one thing, above all else that I just can't seem to process is the term *lung cancer*. I mean,

I *know* that I have cancer. I've accepted that and am taking the proper precautions to make sure it doesn't spread and I'm lying on this bed, plugged into this beeping machine that's lowering chemicals into my body and probably killing my kidneys and I gave up my testicle and what's that now? Lung cancer? Did I mention that my wife is outside smoking a cigarette while I'm being told this?

"Yes. Lung cancer. There are several dark spots," and I say, "Several like three?" and I can feel my voice starting to crack and there's nothing I can do to control it. There is, in fact, nothing I can do to control anything. I wipe my nose with my hand and pretend that I'm just wiping "casual snot" away and not "crying snot."

"I'm not exactly sure. A lot. Maybe 17 of various sizes."

And then he stands up and says, "But this," and he signals to my IV bag, "should take care of it. You should probably be fine."

Probably.

And then, without saying goodbye, he leaves and I am alone.
Alone.

The reality show plays on mute and I stare at the TV but I don't see anything. My vision goes blurry and my nose starts to run and tears stream down my cheeks and my head slumps down and *it* has broken me one week in and—

The doctor pokes his head back in, the way someone might pop back in to say, "Did I leave my keys here?" but instead of inquiring about a misplaced item, says, "Oh, sorry. I forgot to mention, there are also spots on your heart," and then, like that, he disappears.

I'm sitting hunchbacked, head tilted down, tears dropping onto my groin in such quantity that it's actually looking like I've pissed this stupid blue robe. My wife enters and says, "What's wrong? Are you OK? What happened?" and I say, "I have lung cancer and heart cancer. I have stage four cancer," and I sob and take a breath and say, "Do you know how high those numbers go?" and Jade is silent so I say, "Four. They only go to four."

I believe the human spirit can evolve through nearly anything and, given enough time, most things about cancer even become routine and expected. Months and months down the road, the brokenness and isolation and hopelessness will be old hat but today it is brand new. Today I've been told that my cancer is twice as strong as it was when I walked in the door. Today the hopelessness is fresh and new and horrific. My wife and I are twenty-four and twenty-six, respectively, and I'm wondering if I only have months to live and my wife is wondering if she'll be a widow before her twenty-fifth birthday. We wonder how far this can go. How deep is this hole? How dark is this blackness? And we wonder it all in silence as we squeeze each other's hands and shoulders and we both stare at our feet and we shut our eyes and we gasp and sob, confronted by the potential of personal death here and now.

The sun goes down as I'm left wondering what I'll think of Cancer once I'm on the other side, in Remission. I try to imagine how it will look when I'm standing much further away. How will it change me? *Will* it change me?

But yes, I already know the answer to that. When I come out the other side, I will be something altogether new and transformed. I already know that I'll never be the same. I already know that Cancer is my chrysalis, and when it cracks open, something that flies will emerge.

Jade lies on the bed next to me and runs her hand through my beard and says, "I'm going to quit smoking," and I can smell the stale cigarettes on her fingertips. She doesn't stand up and dramatically march to the garbage can, throwing her soft pack of Parliament Lights 100s into the trash. She doesn't make a declaration of Cold Turkey. She doesn't even immediately denounce her nicotine habit that has lasted her a pack a day every day since she was sixteen. Instead she just says, "I'm going to quit smoking," and I believe her and one week later, she does. She snuffs out her final cigarette, leaving me to wonder how many years my cancer has purchased her . . . this thing that's killing me is saving her. I wonder about Cancer and alternative purposes or "Higher Purposes" or silver linings. Call it whatever you want. It's all the same. Bad news with happy endings.

Drip-drip-drip.

822-821-820.

I think about dying and death and cemeteries and morgues and morticians and corpses being embalmed. I think about the blood being sucked out and some foreign chemical being pumped back in so as to preserve the host.

Drip-drip-drip.

809-808-807.

Someone comes in to take my blood out of my body and away to a lab. Someone else comes in and gives me new chemo, some chemical pumping into my body to preserve the host.

Alive or dead, I am a corpse.

CHAPTER 18
INTERMISSION

I have spent my last half a week curled up in a ball trying to sleep away the days so that I could just hurry and get to my nights to sleep more. Vomiting has become as commonplace as blinking, and because personal hygiene is the very last thing on my mind, I haven't showered or brushed my teeth in something like ninety-six hours.

I keep telling Jade that I'm sick and she keeps telling the nurse that I'm sick and the nurse keeps bringing nausea medication but it never works. It's like taking Tylenol because your leg just got ripped off. The sickness has grown and amplified and magnified, no longer a harmless garden variety lizard but now a towering reptilian monster destroying various major cities that are, symbolically, each of my organs.

My "hangover" has matured into a full-fledged Death Bed Shutdown where I don't *feel* pain; I *am* pain. It radiates from the center of my body, at a point where my ribs and lungs meet. I can feel my diaphragm; I can feel the meat and bone surrounding it. I can feel every inch of tissue, every cell, every strand of DNA, flowing with black hatred. My heart pumps blood and my stomach churns food and my lungs circulate oxygen and this spot in my chest produces pain, sending it out in waves, reaching into the furthest extremities of my limbs. My eyeballs throb and the light is blinding and sickening and overwhelming, every bright color a dart to the back of my skull. Every noise is sent through a megaphone placed against my ear. The television, the radio, the beeping of my IV machine, footsteps, toilets flushing, birds chirping, everything hits my brain like a bare-knuckled super soldier. Pliers twist and grind inside my head, and my stomach feels like an ocean filled with buttery fat, wave after wave of sloshy curdled goop washing onto my shores. I puke into the buttery waves and the world screams at me and the pain pinches my eyes and blasts through my body and I am on fire, filled with poison, my body shoving chemicals in and out, in and out, my liver screaming like a witch at the pyre.

The Black Tendrils are slowly dying, curling back like a rose bush in winter solstice, but a new monster is rising up, something worse than cancer, something without a face or a cure. Because it *is* the cure. This is not the cancer making me sick. This is the medicine making me sick.

I make earnest prayers to God to please just let me die. I am in so much pain. Every ounce of energy I have stored is being pulled away from me. Everything is a fight. Everything is a battle. Walking, talking, eating, chewing, shitting, blinking, breathing, it's all one vicious fight after the next. My life is a *Faces of Death* segment played in super slow motion.

My stomach hurts so badly that I feel as though I can't stand up. Every movement I make, no matter how small or subtle, upsets my senses like a boat in the ocean, capsizing it and drowning the crew. I lie as still as possible for as long as possible and think about how the doctor told me that the treatments will compound, that they'll become worse every time.

This is just the beginning and I am at the end of my rope.

Never before or since have I felt such pain as that which plagued me through chemotherapy. I cry often and often I cry alone. I shut my eyes and see the flame of hope flickering, threatening to extinguish. The proverbial light at the end of the tunnel is far away, through a maze of subterranean tubes, and out of sight, out of mind. I'm in the desert and my ending is a slow burn. I can't imagine ever coming out of this, ever being healthy, ever being *unsick*. I can't see past the next moment in time, the next bag of chemo, the next dose of medicine.

The pain builds and grows inside me with every passing moment, a thermometer rising, the mercury inside of it threatening to burst out in a spray of toxicity.

On Monday, I tell Jade that I want to die. On Tuesday, I repeat myself. On Wednesday, I say it again until I absolutely believe it. On Thursday, I just keep mumbling it over and over like a mantra, begging the darkness to swallow me up. Tiny violins play wherever I go. On Friday, Jade sits down next to me and says, "Is that really what you want? To die?" and I look at my feet, ashamed and feeling stupid all

147

of a sudden. She repeats herself but I don't answer. She tells me that I'm not going through this alone. She tells me that I'm not alone. She tells me—and I cut her off. I say, "I *am* alone. *I'm* the one in the hospital bed. *I'm* the one with the IV stuck in my arm. *I'm* the one with the pain in my bones and the fear in my brain—" and now it's her turn to cut me off. She says, "You're not going through this alone. You might be carrying the pain around but I'm twenty-four years old and I have to sit aside and watch my husband die . . . and the worst part is he's just going right along without even swinging a punch. Where's your fight?" and then she lets that thought hang in the air like rotten fruit.

She takes my hand in hers and rubs her thumb along the ridge of my plain, gold wedding band. "It's loose," she says, and I look down. Even my fingers are losing weight. I shrug. She slides my ring off my finger and silently reads the inscription that runs around its inside, hidden from view. She laughs and says, "I remember when I took this ring to the jeweler to have it engraved. There was a really old woman behind the counter and she told me to write down exactly, *exactly* what I wanted it to say. When I handed her the paper, her face," Jade laughs. "Her mouth dropped open and her eyes popped out and she goes, 'Is this a joke?' And I say, 'Nope.' And the woman says, 'This is for a wedding ring?' and I told her it was for my husband to-be. She had this look that was like, *Young people . . . .* Then," she continues, "I remember on our wedding day, we walked down the aisle, just married and, in the

148

backroom, waiting to be announced outside for the rice throwing, I told you to take it off and read it. Do you remember?"

And yes, I do remember. I gave it a tug and it came off easy that day, as well, from my nervous-sweaty hands. I held the shining circle up to the light, tilted it just so and read the following words, laid out in all caps: WE'RE NOT GONNA MAKE IT.

If I had any doubts about marrying the right girl, they vanished right there.

Jade now, in real time, in the hospital, three years into our marriage, slides the ring back onto my finger and says, "We *are* going to make it. Both of us. You stop telling yourself otherwise."

I say, "OK," and, "I know," and, "You're right," and, while I quit saying those things and while I try hard to stop thinking them, they still rattle around in the dark recesses of my brain, cluttering it and infecting it.

I reach my hand out and hold hers, rubbing my thumb against the back of her palm until the nurse enters to remove my IV because, thank God so very, very much, today is the day we're leaving.

The nurse at hand struggles with removing the IV thanks to the massive amounts of tape that had been used to set it to my arm. She apologetically pulls and tugs at the sticky material, tearing out countless arm hairs while ruthlessly jerking the catheter tube that rests in my vein in and out, in and out. I bite my bottom lip and my eyes pinch shut. The nurse picks at the tape with her fingernail and rips another strip off with a drawn out, "Sohhhhh-ryyyyy," and a grimace.

When she finally manages to pull out the tube, I experience a sensation that I can only equate to that which you feel after jumping off of a trampoline, the way the ground feels foreign and strange. After eight days of the constant tug of the pole and tubes I feel like a part of me is missing.

By policy I'm not allowed to walk to the exit myself so I'm asked to sit in a wheelchair while my wife escorts me. I feel humiliated every time we pass someone in the hall even though I know the emotion is stupid and senseless.

One week after beginning my six-month treatment, I am released from the hospital and allowed to go home for an *intermission*—two weeks of down time before I return for my second interval.

When we get in the car, I lie down in the backseat and shut my eyes. On the forty-minute drive home I feel every single bump in the freeway, every pothole, every stomp of the brake. I feel everything, my senses not numbed but amplified. I am a glass of liquid, waiting to spill.

I ask Jade to turn down the music and she does but then I ask her to shut it off completely. I put

150

my hands over my ears and can't imagine this getting any worse. I ask her to pull over and I puke into the gutter twice.

We get home and I sit down in a soft yellow rocking chair, a piece of furniture that my wife and I found abandoned under a bridge when we first moved to LA. It seemed like it was in good enough condition so we brought it home.

Like a good dog, it's been well loved.

Severe chills run up and down my body so I put on a thick hoodie, pull up the hood and give the strings a good tug, scrunching my field of vision. I shut my eyes and try to sleep but to no avail.

My mom asks if we feel like playing that popular board game *Sorry!* and my wife says sure and I say nothing but sit at the table and stare at the board. I roll the die—

—die—

—and move my marker and roll my die and move my marker and die and Cancer Marker.

I sit back in my chair and Jade asks what I want for dinner and I tell her I'm not hungry. My stomach hurts. I puke again, this time simply at the thought of food being placed on my tongue.

The hospital has sent us home with a small suitcase filled with pharmaceuticals: two kinds of anti-nausea pills, several pain relievers for head, several pain relievers for body, stool softeners because the pain relievers cause constipation; vitamins A through F, K through P and R, V and Z individually. My mother has also personally prescribed fish oil and ginkgo biloba, which I think is for memory loss but I can't exactly recall.

Lying in bed that night, I stare at the fan blades spinning round and wonder how many times they've turned since I've lived in this house. Ten thousand? A hundred thousand? I start counting but only get to seven when my wife reaches over and gives me a kiss on my cheek.

I turn to her and she says, "Hey," and I say, "Hey," and, because I realize that I *still* haven't brushed my teeth in over a week now, I sort of avert my mouth.

She places her hand on my stomach and says, "Hey," and raises an eyebrow and I say, "Uh . . . " and, even though I've promised myself to "be strong" the thought that keeps rolling through my head is, "I just want to die, I just want to die, I just want to die," but instead I say, "Is this, like, sympathy sex?" and she laughs and says that she digs guys with cancer.

I smile and give her a kiss on the cheek and we try our very best but the entire time I'm just fighting my gag reflex from the constant rocking and my bones feel like they're going to crumble and for some reason I keep picturing my dick as raw butcher meat and I am just totally worthless and there's no way this is happening.

Cancer: the ultimate cock block.

I eventually say, "I . . . I can't do this," and lie back on the bed and say, "Sorry," and she says, "It's OK, I'm really into guys that are emotionally and physically damaged."

We hold hands and I tickle her back and she goes to sleep and I continue to count, "Eight . . . nine . . . ten . . . ."

CHAPTER 19
300

I wake up outside, my back sore from the wrought iron chair I've fallen asleep in. My mother has been insisting that I need to get more vitamin D and so I keep heading to the back yard and passing out. This is before I had a smart phone – back when my flip phone was still the rage. No fun games while I sit around. There is only staring into the distance and contemplating the mundane.

I shuffle back inside, sit back in my yellow chair and think about time passing, oceans turning to deserts, rocks turning to sand, babies turning to men turning to dust.

On a bored whim I decide to write my boss to tell him what's been happening to me and how thankful I am that he's saving my job until I get back. He responds and says that someone is filling in for me temporarily and that I should "get well soon," a sentiment that I always find painfully cheap and obvious.

Oh, you're sick? Get well soon. Don't stay sick! The sooner you can get back to health, the better! That's what I always say! Look! I've even had it inscribed onto this delightful commemorative Mylar balloon!

In any event, the part about my job being there raises my spirits. Our money is sinking fast and we're going to need some serious dough when we come out the other side of this made-for-TV original movie. The nest egg I'd set aside to make my feature film has become our landing pad, our safety net, our buffer. It's the only thing separating us from total and complete bankruptcy. The money is not going into camera rentals and crew; it's going into food and rent and electricity. It is our life source and umbilical cord to survival.

A few days later, my dad leaves to head back to South Dakota and his job and real life. He gives me that awkward side hug again and then goes to bed saying, "I'm leaving around four in the morning so I probably won't see you again." He disappears around the corner and I wonder if he thinks about how heavy those words sound.

He and my mother had had a previous conversation a few nights prior wherein they'd discussed her staying with us, operating as third eyes and extra hands; helping, supporting, cooking, cleaning, anything, everything; watching me while Jade went to work, entertaining Jade while I slept. She helps keep sanity, helps us keep a link to the outside world. We both welcome the idea with open arms and for six months my mother left her husband, her own mother, her brothers and sisters. My family is very close and my mother has her helping hands in a lot of pies back home and for half a year she left everyone. She quit her job and stopped her life to come sit by Jade and me and suffer with us.

Let this be a true example of a mother's love. She gave everything she had.

She takes up residence in our guest bedroom and it's the first piece of good news we've had in some time. Her presence is an absolute godsend because, I don't care how old you are, there is something inherently primitive and wonderful about having your mother around. Mothers are, after all, the original chicken soup for the soul.

So on those days when I just feel like I am the world's last unicorn and am shedding a tear of sorrow for my lost species, she is there to make me feel just a little bit better. Fly, unicorn, fly.

*** *** *** *** ***

It's either a Monday or a Thursday and it's either 11 a.m. or 4 p.m. The sun rises and sets and the clock spins and resets and day and night keep changing places like characters in a David Lynch film. Without a job or any regular routine, time becomes irrelevant. I sit in my chair, glossy eyed, and listen to my mother and wife talk about dogs and work and God and recipes and marriage and cotton, the fabric of our lives.

I lean forward and stand up on legs that feel atrophied after only a couple weeks of inactivity and wobble into the guest bedroom and collapse onto the bed.

I bury my face in a pillow, shut my eyes and pray for a miraculously healing. But nothing happens. I'm still sick.

I fall asleep and an undisclosed amount of time passes wherein I wake, cramped and sweaty, vomit, fall back to sleep, kick off the blankets, find I'm chilled, vomit, roll over, wish I were dead, regret my weakness, and then fall back to sleep.

When I wake, I find a short, curly hair stuck in my mouth and, for once, I don't gag from the chemo. An image of my father's naked body crosses my mind, his thick shoulders pressed into this very mattress, his back hair dropping off him and resting dormant until I vacuum them into my gaping face hole.

I am eating my father's back hair.

Gag.

Quicker than I've moved in weeks, I sit up and see that my pillow is covered in them; easily twenty hairs populate the upper mattress area and I make a note to ask my mom if Dad sheds often.

I sit up and place my feet firmly on the floor—as firmly as I'm able to—and stare at myself in the full-length closet mirror. I'm still me but . . . a little thinner. It's only been two weeks but, like a newborn with an eating disorder, I only consume very delicate portions, unable to hold anything down. The bags that I always carry with me under my eyes are suddenly starting to look a little darker, a little heavier, less like bags and more like luggage for a long cross-country road trip. I sigh and rub my chin and when I look at my hand, my stomach leaps into my throat.

My palm is covered in hundreds of short, tight hairs. Hairs that look exactly like the ones on the mattress. My hair. My beard. It's falling out. In large chunks.

I reach up, grab a handful of beard in my hand, and gently pull. Like a ten-year-old on a greased up Slip 'N Slide, my hair slides out of my follicles and away from my face. No tug, no pluck, no tension. Yanking grass from the Earth would put up a better fight. My hair had, for all intents and purposes, suddenly just given up.

I shout for Jade, and when she enters the room, I hold out my hand and she says, "What . . . . Oh . . . . " We both stare at my hand in silence for a moment, both of us thinking about bald kids coughing blood into Kleenexes.

"My hair is falling out," I say and my wife nods and her eyes well up a little. "Do you want to . . . shave it?" and I nod.

159

It takes less than three days for my eyebrows, armpit, and pubic hair to follow suit. I look, in short, like one of those hairless Egyptian cats but with less sex appeal.

The next day is dreary and overcast as we drive into my bi-weekly oncology checkup. Sitting in the cold office, Dr. Yen asks me a series of inquiries, listens to my heart, takes my blood and asks if I have any questions.

I say, "I'm always cold."

She says, "That's normal."

I say, "Will this go away?"

She says, "Probably not."

I say, "Ever?"

She says, "Never."

I say, "I feel like shit."

She says, "That's normal."

I say, "Will this go away?"

She says, "Someday. I told you. Mack Truck."

My wife says, "He's really depressed."

The doctor says, "I have a pill for that."

My blood count comes back from the lab and the results are grim; my red count is too low, which essentially amounts to me being filled to the brim with bad blood. Imagine putting gas in your car that's been cut with water. Or perhaps an even more accurate analogy would be to say, "Imagine putting water in your body that's been cut with gasoline."

On the oncologist's command, we drive straight from her office to the hospital for a platelet transfusion. My white blood count is too low, as well, leaving my body weak and defenseless, able to be killed (very literally) by a common cold. Every sneeze is a bullet.

The nurse who comes in to give me my IV is a middle-aged Asian woman who, when questioned, claims she is The Best EYE-VEE-Giver this hospital has and that I am lucky to have her. This immediately puts my mind at ease.

She sticks the 2-inch needle into my forearm and I slam my eyes closed like iron-blast doors and wiggle my toes and imagine I'm in Norway and then she lets go of me and I say, "That was fast," but she says, "I couldn't find a vein," and when I open my eyes she's still holding the needle in her hand.

I rest my head back on the pillow and she begins tapping around my bicep. "There we go. There's a good one," she says and I close my eyes again as the silver thread sneaks under my skin and sniffs around for its— "Oops—OK—I just blew your vein. I'm really sorry. One more time."

I turn my head aside and fight back a scream of terror as the knife gets thrust into my forearm a third time at an awkward angle and is taped down. "Bingo!" she shouts, and I jokingly/seriously say, "The best, huh?" and she says, "Well, the best intern."

She exits, and I sigh while my mother and wife play *Yahtzee*. Moments later, the intern returns with a bag of milky glue and hangs it from my IV pole. Then, like a crazy straw being set into the world's grossest milkshake, she inserts my IV tube into the bag and the cummy sludge gloops and glops down into my veins . . . for 12 hours.

I watch the drizzling cream leak into me and wonder who it belonged to—a starving college student, a man on the brink of poverty, an immigrant, some Good Samaritan who makes monthly donations? From their body to mine, they don't know it, but they're helping me, saving me, pulling me out of the red and into the black. I'm still sick. I'm still hopeless. I'm still depressed. I still want to stick my head in the microwave. But . . . sitting up in bed, I do suddenly feel a small surge of energy idly pulsing through me. It's not a forest fire. But it is a spark.

The nurse comes back with an update on my HCG levels, those cancer markers that had sky rocketed from 300 to 900. Today, she tells me that they've dropped back to 300.

Three hundred.

The cancer is dying. It's fighting, but it's dying. And it is here that I shut my eyes and see that spark flicker and grow a little brighter. I'm going to win. I'm going to choke you to death, you son of a bitch. You're going to pull me down to the swamps of disease and despair and I'll follow along until you're neck deep in whatever primordial muck you've come from and then, at the last moment, I'll pull the trigger and cut you free and you'll sink away back into those vile depths.

I open my eyes and watch a television show about a man who gets a face transplant after being mauled by a bear.

I have no real problems.

CHAPTER 20
RLS

It's Wednesday or Sunday and it might be getting close to noon because I can hear *Dr. Oz* promos on the television. I'm lying on the bathroom floor, staring at the pipes behind the toilet and wondering how many gallons have gone through them. I try to imagine how much water is used in one flush and how many flushes my city block goes through in a day and I try to imagine how many flushes it would take to empty the ocean.

My mother pokes her head in and asks me if I've taken my fish oil today and I say, "No," and she lowers her hand to me. Ask and you shall receive. Fish oil. I stick it in my mouth, gag, drink water, gag, puke, and put the pill in the toilet. My mom says, "Can I get you anything?" and I say, "My wife."

Jade enters a few minutes later and I say, "I want to try cannabis. If it doesn't work and it doesn't make a difference, then fine, I'll stop, but these pills aren't working and it's all bullshit. I keep puking the anti-puking pills up and the pain in my body makes me want to stick a gun in my mouth."

She sits down on the floor with me, pulls out her smart phone and begins punching something in. A few moments later she says, "There's a doctor in Hollywood. We can schedule you an appointment today—" and I say, "I can just call Bernard. He'll hook us up," and her face goes red and she says,

165

"Listen to me! I'm not dealing with cancer *and* a pot head. If we're doing this medically then you need to be responsible about it and only take it when you need it. OK?" and I say, "Oh-kay," and she says, "And if I ever hear you use the term *wake and bake* we're done, *OK?*" and I say, "Yes, oh-*kay*," and she hits the call button on the phone and schedules me an appointment for tomorrow early afternoon.

That night, like the last ten days, I sleep a total of forty-five minutes in scattered and broken chunks. I lie in bed and stare at the ceiling and stare at the fan and smell the blankets and touch my wife's back and sometimes I cry. I just sit in the dark, in the silence and let tears run down my face and feel sorry for myself and then I call myself a pussy and tell myself to man up. The hatred I feel for my own weakness is palpable.

I feel so alone.

The sensation of needing to stretch my legs washes over me and so I push them out but it doesn't go away. I crunch them up to my body and then try again but still the feeling abides. This is restless leg syndrome, RLS, something I would have thought was a total joke—some new-age medical Make Believe to help sell over the counter, bottled placebos—until I had it myself and it kept me from sleeping.

I shut my eyes and the sensation washes through me and so I wiggle my toes but it just digs in deeper. I move my ankles from side to side and then

166

roll over onto my stomach and bury my head under a pillow, my preferred method of sleep.

I'm out . . .and I'm just starting to dream . . . and then I'm awake again and the sensation is back and so I lift one leg in the air. My wife wakes up and asks, "Are you all right?" and I say, "I think I have RLS—that's, uh—restless leg syndrome," and then, because I think it somehow makes it more legitimate, I say, "It's a real thing, you know," and she says, "Uh-huh," and then I can hear her heavy sleep-breathing again.

Finally, exhausted and angry, I stand up on restless legs and give them what they want—a short walk into the living room where I find myself craving Cinnamon Toast Crunch, one of the only things I find I can actually stomach, even in small quantities.

I pour myself a huge bowl—sixteen toasts deep—grab my copy of Bret Easton Ellis's *American Psycho*, and throw myself down in My Yellow Chair. For the next two-and-a-half hours, I skim pages, trying to fight my way to the end of Patrick Bateman's free-flowing, psychotic narrative.

It's the last book I'll be able to read until The End.

Finally, hearing birds chirping outside the window, I decide to make my way back to bed, lie down, and shut my eyes. When I wake up, it's morning and my wife is getting ready for work. She tells me that my appointment with the weed doctor is at 2:30 and she's emailed me the address and then says, "I did some research and I think our best bet is going to be to get you a vaporizer because it's the cleanest—*cleanest, honestly*—way to go. Better than joints," and I say, "I'm fine with buying a pipe," and she says, "*JOHN, NO*. Do you hear what I'm saying? It's cleaner. It's *cleaner,* whatever that means. You have *lung*—did you just space out?" and I say, "Yeah."

Space out, zone out, daze out—this is what we call the absent seizures I've had since I was a kid. My eyes roll back in my head for a few seconds, taking me out of reality, before I suddenly snap back, aware that something strange has happened. I don't fall down or convulse; I simply . . . blank out. I was diagnosed in seventh grade, and after literally years and years of trial and error with different seizure medications, the doctors and neurologists were finally able to peg a specific cocktail that eradicated my seizures completely without causing mood swings or stomachaches. The medication keeps them tame and at bay but they tend to make special guest appearances when I'm really tired or when I don't take my pills. Which I haven't because I simply throw them up. Which I am because I have RLS and haven't been sleeping. I tell her this and she says, "Well, knock it off—start taking your pills. Why are you messing around with this?" and I say, "I *PUKE. THEM. UP.* I can't swallow anything! You think I want to be spacing out like—"

168

"It just happened again! Take your pills!" and she storms out of the room and comes back with a pill. I take it and she leaves and I lie in bed for the next twenty minutes, trying to keep it down.

Eventually, I lose and watch the little red capsule float, half dissolved, in the toilet.

When I walk into the kitchen, my mom asks me how I slept and I say, "I think I have RLS," and she says, "Oh, nooooo. What is that?" and I try to explain it but just give up because it sounds so stupid rolling out of my mouth.

She asks if I want any breakfast and I tell her that a 10 oz. steak and eggs would be nice. She chuckles and takes a sip of her coffee while I ask her, a traditionally conservative person, what she thinks about this "marijuana thing". She smiles and says, "If it helps, it helps." It's the closest thing she's going to say to, "Go smoke weed, dear." I nod and smile.

The TV rolls on and on with various daytime television shows and I watch the shadows shrink on the floor as the sun shifts across the sky (or, as I go hurtling past it in space) and I think about the journey in front of me; not just the one I'm taking into Hollywood today but the whole journey, The Cancer Journey. I wonder what the next few rounds are going to do to my body. I'm already sore and depressed and weak. I try to imagine how it could possibly be worse. I feel like a cat in some animal-testing factory; locked in a cage and forced to undergo experiments until I either, ultimately, live or die.

I wonder what That Guy is doing in my edit bay at work right now, not thinking about a thing, making my money, working on my projects, sitting in my chair, eating cookies from Cookie Dave that are supposed to be mine and wondering what he's going to eat for lunch while I eat nothing and—

—space out.

Thanks to the chemo, I'm freezing everywhere I go so it's not unusual for me to be wearing a long-sleeved thermal, then a T-shirt, then a sweater, then a light jacket with a scarf and beanie underneath a large winter parka designed for South Dakota blizzards, fuzzy hood pulled up and covering my face. I'm constantly shivering, an army of goose bumps standing at full attention around the clock like fleshy militia men, my nipples always fully erect and easily 7s on the mineral hardness scale. I live and die in these clothes. In my chair, in the car, in bed, in the hospital, this is what I'm wearing, bundled up like a baby chick in a cotton incubator.

My mom puts on a light jacket over her T-shirt and grabs her car keys while I sit in my chair, ready to take on life. As long as life doesn't entail anything more exhausting or hazardous than sleeping. "You ready to go?" she asks and I say, "This is me. Anything that happens—this is what you get. It isn't much but it's all I have," and she says, "Come off it," and I roll off the chair and lie on the ground and say, "I want to buy a wheelchair," but when I look up she's already walked out the door.

We stop at a gas station to fill up and my mom asks me if I want anything. I tell her that a Yoo-hoo is sounding about right, and when she brings two out, I drink the first all in one long hit like a wino slamming a 40 of Olde E. I can't help it; it's just so delicious. Nothing has felt so sweet and refreshing on my palate for . . . how long?

We get on the road and I crack the second Yoo-hoo, get through half of it, and then ask her to kindly pull over the car. I open the door and puke up delicious "chocolate drink". This activity has become so regular that my mom doesn't even ask if I'm all right anymore. Instead she just starts flipping through radio stations, trying to find something that sounds like The Jackson 5.

I shut the door and put my seatbelt back on and just nod and she puts the car into drive and away we go. This is chemo shorthand.

Now, it should be said that my mother is not one for driving in big cities. On family vacations while growing up, it was typically my father who would sit behind the wheel, navigating us down congested freeways and through strange cities, and even now, as an adult, whenever my parents travel together, it is my dad who drives.

So, having my mother live with us for six months was going to require her to acclimate to highways and on-ramps and carpool lanes and aggressive drivers and traffic jams and tailgaters and honking and all the horrible things that come along with big cities.

She's white knuckling the steering wheel, cruising down the 101, driving in the far right lane as slow as the law allows, cars flying past in the other four lanes and honking. "What do they *want*?" she asks me and I say, "I think they want you to break 45," and she says, "I'm comfortable here," and I say, "I'm comfortable here, as well."

I look at my phone and read her the directions, "In three-quarters of a mile you're going to take the Highland Boulevard exit. The road is going to sort of bend around and then force you onto Cahuenga, but it becomes Highland—here it is—just keep following that white car—see how the road—"

And then my mind and body, without warning, completely shut down.

CHAPTER 21
PRESIDENT BUSH

When I wake up, the first thing I notice is a group of trees in the distance, far away and small. Maybe pines? The second thing I notice are innumerable cars racing back and forth between myself and the trees. The third thing I notice is a man I've never seen before hovering over me in a blue suit. He's holding my shoulder and telling me to relax.

I breathe slowly and deliberately and try to look around. Standing on the sidewalk is my mother, her eyes red and glassy, her hands shaking; another, slightly heavier man, stands next to the first, also wearing a blue suit—no, not a suit. A uniform. I turn my head and see a red truck—an ambulance. Paramedics.

The man with his hand on my shoulder tells me to take it easy and to have a seat and I see for the first time that the heavy man has a wheelchair. I get out of the car—Whose car is this?—and sit in the wheelchair—How did I get here?—and the heavy man kicks a switch and the wheelchair reclines and the feet kick out and, just like that, I'm on a stretcher.

I have no idea where I am or why. I have no idea where I was going or where I was coming from or what happened to me in between the two and it isn't until this very moment that I remember that I don't remember anything. My past is abyss; just blank space that rolls into the horizon.

The men push me into the back of the ambulance and I say, "What's—I'm sorry—what's happening?" and the main paramedic, crawling in behind me says, "You had a grand mal seizure, and your mom called 911. Can you tell me what year it is?" and I say, "2001," and he says, "OK, it's 2008, Johnny," and I cock my head to the side feeling as though I've had nearly a decade of time stolen away from me. *Where have I been? What was lost?* And he says, "Can you tell me who the president is?" and I say, "Bush—President George Bush," and the paramedic says nothing, so I say, "Am I right?" and he says, "The President is Barack Obama," and I shut my eyes. *What is happening to my brain? Don't take my brain! Don't take my brain! It's all I have! My nuts are gone, my health is gone, my HAIR is gone! Leave my brain!*

He says, "Do you know where you live?" and I stare at the paramedic . . . and then I look out the back doors . . . and I hold my breath, feeling like if I just buy some time I can find the answer. If I just have a moment to rummage around in my memory banks I can pull it up and then they'll know that I'm not as sick as they think; this was all just a mistake. I know it's there, the information, somewhere. I sigh and say, "Somewhere . . . in the Valley . . . " and he says, "Do you know who your wife is?" and I say with complete confidence, "Jade Brookbank. My wife's name is Jade Brookbank."

It's the only thing I can remember.

The doors swing shut behind me and I find myself in a claustrophobic steel box, the paramedic leaning over me. I shut my eyes and just can't believe this is happening. Everything is getting worse.

The paramedic turns and comes back with an oxygen mask that he tries to place over my mouth but I brush him away and say, "No—no oxygen," and he says, "It's OK, just relax," and tries to put it over my mouth again. There's some light in the back of my brain, some glimmer of a memory; I hear a doctor saying, "The bleomycin will effect your lungs—you can't have pure oxygen—it will damage the lining. You can't scuba dive, you can't have oxygen masks," and so I brush it away again. The paramedic raises an eyebrow at me and I say, "I can't have it—it'll hurt me," and he says, "Everything is OK, just—" and he tries to put it on one more time but then, behind him, The Mother Bear comes to the rescue of her cub.

"STOP!" and the paramedic looks over and she says, "He can't *have* it," and the paramedic slowly puts down the mask and says, "Oh, uh, ok . . . . "

He gives me an IV while I have a panic attack, seat belts me in/straps me to a slab, takes a seat, and says to the driver, "Hit it," while spinning his finger in the air.

The driver/heavy paramedic twists the key, flips a switch, and punches the gas. The cherries flash on, the sirens wail, and I feel the ambulance drop off the curb and then blow 70 miles an hour down the freeway.

We're at the Burbank hospital in a matter of minutes. The paramedics wheel me inside and leave me in a hallway, pressed against a wall on my gurney, alone. I stare at the ceiling, feeling out of place, while various patients and visitors walk past me; I'm a sideshow or a misplaced trinket. Where is my wife? Where is my *mother*?

I wonder if she's gotten lost somewhere in the city, unable to find her way out of the rat's nest that is Hollywood, and then time bends and refracts and they're both suddenly at my side. My mother, she wraps her trembling fingers around my skeletal hand and kisses me and says, "You scared your ol' mama, little man," and I realize then that it's how she still sees me—just her little boy who she raised from birth, now lying in front of her, looking like the recently dead rather than the slowly dying, my weight dropping, my eyes sinking, my cheeks going sallow and pale. She sees a little boy on a tricycle with white hair, straight as straw. She sees a little boy on his first day of school, crying and afraid. She sees the little boy who used to sneak into his mother and father's bedroom at night and sleep on the floor at the foot of the bed. No matter how old I become, she will forever see me stuck in time and now Cancer is poisoning that child and those memories for her.

She tells me that we were chatting on the freeway, taking the exit, taking the bend and then my head hit my knees and I curled into a tight ball and began to growl.

I say, "*What?*" and she says, "At first I thought you were just being *John Lowell* and trying to be funny but then you didn't stop and you started leaning into me," and I say, "*What*?" and she says, "I just put my arm out and tried to hold you back—you had your seat belt on but . . . I came off that exit and there was no shoulder and nowhere to pull off, I didn't know what to do. As soon as I saw a sidewalk I just pulled onto it and stopped."

"You drove on the sidewalk?" and she says, "I didn't *drive* on it. I *parked* on it—and I was terrified. John, I don't know where I am. I just started praying to God for help—you were—I don't even know—and I don't know where I was and—I called 911 and they asked where I was and I couldn't see any street signs and I couldn't remember the name of the exit we just took and then . . . a little family of angels showed up," and I say, "A whole family?" and she says, "A mini-van pulled up behind me and a man and a woman got out and approached me and asked if I was all right. I told them what I could and then the man took the phone from me and spoke to the dispatcher . . . and then they waited with me until the ambulance arrived. One of them held your hand while the other one held your head. They were my little angels that Jesus sent."

I say, "Well. At least I wasn't driving," and my mother says, "John *Lowell*. Yes, at least. I swear."

A nurse pushes me into a side room, closes the curtain around us, and says a doctor will be with us shortly. The doctor enters and says something about my absent seizures or *petite mal seizures*; the little space outs that I have. He says they're caused when one little part of my brain misfires. *Petite*, little.

But he says that, depending on a number of factors (lack of sleep and not taking the prescribed dosage of medication among them) that one misfire can signal a second can signal a third and so on and so forth until it grabs an entire section of my brain, effectively causing a *grand mal seizure*. *Grand*, big.

He tells us this *should* be an isolated incident and then my wife says, "He has cancer," and the doctor says, "Cancer?" and he flips through his papers, "What kind of cancer?" and my wife says, "Stage 4. It started with testicular and then turned to lymphoma and now it's in his heart and lungs," and the doctor tries to sell it but he fails. You can see the muscles in his face tighten and his eyes narrow ever so slightly; he's in a spaghetti western standoff and he doesn't want to trigger any alarm from the opposition.

He doesn't say the words but he might as well have shouted them in my ear.

Brain Cancer.

He coughs into his hand and says, "OK, well, we'll just do a CAT scan—very typical for all first-time patients—make sure everything is clear and then—I'll send someone in right now," and then he disappears behind the curtain like a magician after a show.

None of us says a word. My wife holds my left hand and my mother holds my right hand and I shut my eyes and try to picture the tumors that are now probably resting directly behind them, throbbing and rotting away at me.

When I first started dating my wife in high school, her cousin, a seventeen-year-old football player, was fighting a losing battle with brain cancer. The first time I met him he was sitting on a couch, covered in blankets, his eyes nearly closed. His mother said, "Nate, this is Johnny," and I, eighteen at the time and only one year older than this kid, held my hand in the air and said, "Hi." I remember Nate lifting his hand up until it was level with his heart, not even having the strength to tilt the fingers toward the ceiling. They just pointed straight toward me like a salute.

The next time I saw Nate was at his wake.

A male nurse pushes my gurney down to the basement; they stick me inside The Mechanical Donut, push the dye in, make me feel like I've pissed and shit myself, and then wheel me back upstairs and into my room where my mother and wife look as sick as I do.

Two hours.

We wait two hours for the test results to come back with no word from a doctor or nurse or anyone outside of the curtain. There is nothing in our room but the three of us. We talk, speculate, avoid the elephant tumor in the room and wait, all of us silently saying prayers in the back our of minds until finally we are all praying out loud together with words that couldn't possibly contain more faith or desperation. *Please, God. Please, God. Please, God. I can't take it. Please let the tests come back negative. Please, God. Not my brain. Leave me my brain*! And visceral images of me not being cognitive or conscious come to me. An image of me sitting on a couch, covered in blankets, too tired to raise my hand. Me in a coffin, my wife standing over me, weeping. My mother standing over me, weeping. Me, dead. Images of my wife getting married again and me being a story her new husband is told. Me, existing only in photographs and anecdotes and popular paperback book form.

The doctor enters and hands me a piece of paper. I turn it around and see a black and white scan of my brain. Printed across it in large black letters, all caps, is the word NEGATIVE and I choke and say, "Negative—that's good, right? That's good? Do I have brain cancer? *What does this mean*?!" and the doctor says, "You do not have brain cancer," and I just weep in a way that has never overtaken me before or since.

Both my hands are squeezed until my fingers are white and numb and crushed with wonderful pain that I can feel for another day that is mine.

CHAPTER 22
THE RUSSIAN CLOWN

The next day. The 101 Freeway. The Highland exit. My mom drives over a bump in the road and says, "There. That bump. That's when you turned into a little ball. She drives a bit farther, narrating her tale for me. "So I came down here and I couldn't find anything, I mean, where do they expect you to pull off?" and I scan the horizon, trying to find the trees that I saw. She points at a bus stop and says, "There. That's where I parked." I look across the street and see the small grove running parallel with the Hollywood Bowl.

"So crazy," I say and my mom says, "I know." She is talking about the seizure while I'm staring at a man standing on the corner condemning people to hell dressed in an Elmo costume.

We end up deep in the heart of Hollywood, a maze of busy streets and traffic lights to which no freeway leads. Like David Bowie's labyrinth, there are no true shortcuts.

We pull up outside of an unmarked brick building and make our way to the second floor. Inside, everything is from the '70s—the wallpaper, the art, the doorknobs—but not in that good way that is intentional. I enter a small office clad with crusty shag carpet and worn wool couches. "I have an appointment," I say to the young receptionist. She asks me to sign in and have a seat. I pick up a copy of *Lava Lamp Monthly* and flip through the pages. Two other patients, both young males, are seated with me, both of their eyes so red it looks as if they've just left their mothers' funerals.

Both try to casually eyeball me, a twenty-six-year-old bookended by his mother and wife. They glance at me out of the corners of their rose-colored eyes and must think I'm a complete mess, a ghost in clothes, a dead man walking. A heavy oak door opens and someone calls the first boy's name from the revealed darkness. He enters and disappears into shadows, the door slowly swinging closed on its own accord and then ominously clicking shut behind him. I turn back to my magazine and read about the history of lava lamps. Invented by Edward Craven Walker in 1948, began mass production in 1963, originally named the Astro Globe. A few minutes later, the boy exits, staring at a small card. He pockets it and leaves. The second boy's name is called and it's second verse, same as the first. I have just enough time to read about how the largest lava lamp in the world is 4 feet tall and contains 10 gallons of super-secret-lava-formula before the door opens and the second boy exits. I watch him leave and am just amazed at the speed and efficiency of this doctor's office, which, seeing how quickly everything is progressing, really shouldn't be allowed to call these four walls a waiting room.

My name is called—*Brukbag*—and I tell my posse to stand down cuz I'm goin' alone into the shadows. I find what happens next to be so absurd that it borders on satire.

I enter an ominously dark office, lit only by the slightly cracked blinds. An oddly shaped silhouette sits behind the desk and a scruff voice says, "Cum een, cum een." I take this as *Come in* and close the door softly behind me. The figure signals for me, with a bony hand, to sit, and as I do, my eyes adjust and I see what can only be described as a Russian clown impersonating a doctor.

This woman has chunky blonde hair that's been pulled into two ponytails, each spitting off either side of her head. She wears wire-rimmed glasses that magnify her eyes into enormous green watermelons and her make-up looks as though a blind person with Parkinson's applied it. The lipstick smears off the lips and into that unnamed area between mouth and nose, smudging and smearing in large circles a red color so intense that it's nearly neon pink. Her cheeks are flushed with blush, making her look chronically embarrassed. Emerald green circles surround her eyes the color of, well, emeralds, the glasses magnifying her pores, turning molehills into mountains. Her eyebrows are unplucked pubic bushes above her ocular orbs. Her name is Galina.

Sitting at a dinner once, speaking with an eye doctor about graduation statistics, he leaned in close to me and says, "Do you know what they call the medical student who graduates very last in his class?"

Stumped at his riddle, I shrugged, and he said, "Doctor," and then chuckled to himself.

For anyone not versed in the legalities of this protocol, here's how it shakes down. Galina acts as the gatekeeper. It is her job, as a doctor, to examine each patient and decide if they are in need of a medical marijuana license. If she approves of your disease, you pay her your $100, get an ACCEPTED stamp and walk out the door with a license. You then go to a second location (a dispensary) to purchase your medicinal herbal supplements. Scanning her desk, I can't help but notice that there is no REJECTED stamp next to her envelope filled with money.

I sit down and she says, "What . . . eez rong?" I flop a manila envelope puking with doctor's reports onto her desk and say, "Well . . . I have cancer . . . " and she lights up like a Christmas tree. *Someone with a sickness! A real sickness! Finally! I can use THIS*! And she pulls the stethoscope – I'm not kidding – off her neck and, with a bit too much zest, pops out of her chair and signals me to a couch that looks like it belongs in Freud's office.

I lie down and she, nervous as a virgin, says, "I must . . . exameen yoo." She shoves the ear pieces into her head and places the circular plate against my chest. "Breeth . . . yes . . . agein . . . . "

I take a deep breath and think to myself, "This should be good." I let it out and she taps a little hammer on my knee, testing my reflexes. I say, "Do the legs still work, doc?" and she says, "They seem to bee fine."

She sits back behind her desk and says, "Doo yoo dreenk tap water?" and I say, "Yes," and she says, "Thees . . . Thees ees the problem. There is sometheeng called alkaline in tap water. You must not dreenk it. You pay me three hundreed dollers and I will give you filter. Very good," and I say, "I think the problem might be the cancer on my heart . . . and lungs . . . and the lymphoma . . . and the chemo I'm getting. I can't eat," and she says, "Yes, yes, but . . . thees will help. Three hundreed dollers. Plus one hundreed for medical lizence—four hundreed, very cheep. You be well in I say, one, maybe too munths."

I nod and say, "I sort of don't have a job right now so that seems a little steep," and she says, "Two hundreed for Alkaline filter, one hundreed for mari-wona lizence. You cannot find this deel anywhere else," and I say, "I believe that's true. *However*, I am going to have to politely decline," and she sighs and signs the license and hands it over to me. "Yoo come back, you change your mind."

I shake her hand and leave.

CHAPTER 23
YODA'S CANDY

From Hollywood, we drive straight back to the Valley while Jade looks up available dispensaries in our neighborhood. Now that I've got the license, I have to go to the store. And, lo and behold, the herbal supplement business is ah-booming. Jade sticks her phone in front of my face and I see roughly sixty green (coincidence?) dots on the map, making dispensaries in the Valley the only business with more locations than Starbucks and McDonald's combined.

We pull into one down the street from our house that shares a strip-mall parking lot with a thrift store, a Mexican restaurant, and a Laundromat. Jade and I walk in together while my mother waits in the car. Sitting in the corner is a sleeping cop and inside of a bulletproof cage is a young Hispanic kid with a wiry mustache. He says, "Yo," and asks for my papers. I slide my license and ID through the grate and he tells me to take a seat. He says there are only two people allowed in the back at once.

We sit down and I begin to peruse a copy of *High Times*, wondering what I'll discover in the back room of this place. Will there be some mega drug kingpin sitting behind a smoky desk, playing poker and making deals? No. That's ridiculous. I brush the image from my mind. I stare at the cop and wonder how I get his job. He burps and adjusts his hat, sits up, sees me staring at him and nods.

The back door emits an electronic beep and opens. A kid in a Bob Marley shirt walks out, sees the cop, smiles, and exits. In my head I hear him thinking, "Fuck dah po-lice!" They call my name and my wife and I both stand up. The person at the door quickly says, "She stays," and I say, "I—uh—OK." Jade sits back down and I enter a place like I have never dreamed of.

At the back of the room there is a two-tiered glass case that runs 20 feet long, the kind you'd see in a gun store. It's built for displaying goods but always means the same: "We want you to look, but not touch. Please ask for assistance. Please do not lean on glass. Thank you."

I say, "Double-ewe . . . oh . . . double-ewe . . . " and approach the cabinet. Running side by side on both layers for the entire twenty feet are gallon jugs of weed, each jar proclaiming its particular strain: Cotton Candy, Train Wreck, Buddha's Lightning, White Devil. No two alike.

A big man, bulky and firm, with earlobe length hair the texture of grease, smiles and raises his hand, and in a Russian accent says, "*What ails ya, brother*?!" He speaks cleaner than Galina but the hard edges of his mother country are still heard on his T's and D's.

I say, "I have, uh, cancer," and he puts his hands down on the counter and raises his eyebrows and says, verbatim, "*A real patient!*" He signals me close and whispers, "Listen, between you and me, we knock off twenty percent for sick people."

A second door swings open and in walks a squatter, more froggy looking version of Moe from The Three Stooges. He lifts up a black garbage bag filled with marijuana, opens it up, buries his face inside of it and inhales as deeply as he can before shouting, "*I LOVE WEED!*" in a raspy voice.

I look down at the counter and say, "This is pretty, uh, intense. How do I know what to get?" and he says, "Well . . . do you want to, like, have some energy and go mow the lawn or do you want to just become glued to your couch and forget the world exists?"

My true and honest answer is, "*Both! Both! I desperately want both*! Let me mow my lawn *and* forget that the world exists."

I end up buying an eighth of each, a grinder and a vaporizer. He packs each strain into its own bright green prescription bottle (complete with child safety lid), knocks off the 20 percent cancer-kid discount and says, "See you soon and be well. When you come back, you tell me how those treat you. They're gonna be your best buds," and I imagine this is a tag line he uses on everyone although it feels personal and private between us.

I exit the door back to the waiting room and hold up my brown bag to signal Jade that it's time to ride. As I walk past the cop with my pockets stuffed with weed, I can't help but think, "Fuck dah po-lice!"

CHAPTER 24
UP IN THE CLOUDS

The first thing I do when I get home is fire up YouTube to figure out how to use a vaporizer since it didn't come with any proper instructions. A fourteen-year-old with a lisp tells me that it's essentially a large hot plate that slowly heats up the plant versus doing a straight burn with the chemicals in the butane lighter. Again, "cleaner."

I slowly open the childproof cap and stare down at my beautiful green bulbs with orange strands flecked upon them like glitter. I pull one out and place it in the grinder, turning the plant to dust. I pour the remains in the bowl, flip the switch on the device, and wait for optimum heat.

Meanwhile, my mother sits next to me, watching, staring, observing, obvious that she's fascinated by not only the process, but the plant itself. I hand her the pill bottle and say, "Smell." She lifts it to her nose and says, "It's sweet."

I bring the tube from the vaporizer to my mouth, feeling like the caterpillar in *Alice's Adventures in Wonderland* and pull. The first silver strands weave their way up the plastic lining until they're in my mouth and in my throat and in my lungs and I'm lifting off my feet and I'm smiling and I shut my eyes and everything is so good right now.

I think of all the times I've smoked pot with my sister, sitting on her kitchen floor trying to use every magnet letter on the fridge to spell words, phrases like, CREEP GUY CAN'T DANCE and AARON WILL EAT FARTS. We're smoking and listening to No Doubt's "Tragic Kingdom" and playing *Hogan's Alley* on her Nintendo. We're eating fudge. We're talking about being young and growing up and being very overly philosophical about the minutia of life and I open my eyes and my mom is sitting next to me and I say, "I love you, Mom," and it's such a stupid thing to say in that moment because of what's happening but I feel it so strongly and so truly and I just want her to know that I appreciate everything she's doing for us and sacrificing for us to be here and she leans in and gives me a hug and I say, "Thank you. Thank you. I love you," and then I stand up and just start snapping my fingers and bobbing my head. My wife enters the room and says, "What are you doing?" and I say, "I don't know, I just—I just feel so good. I need to dance. *I need to dance! And if you don't dance then you're no friend of mine.*"

Instead of dancing, my wife just stares at me and itches her nose. I say, "It just feels so good to be alive, doesn't it?! It feels so good! The three of us here, doing this together—doing *life* together! Oh, man. Mom, you should move to Los Angeles. You should live here forever! We could turn our garage into a little house. You wouldn't have to sleep on the couch—we could build a little bathroom out there. How great would that be? How great?"

There's no music playing but I'm sliding back and forth on the cheap tile floor in my socks. I turn around and try to moonwalk but it just looks like when everyone *tries* to moonwalk; just me walking backward, sliding the soles of my feet across a dirty floor.

I open up the cabinet and pour myself a big bowl of Cinnamon Toast Crunch and eat the entire thing. I open a drawer and pull out a Butterfinger—the size you'd get in a Halloween handout—and eat two. I drink a glass of water and sit down on a bar stool at the island in my kitchen. I turn to my wife and tell her some stupid joke that both begins and ends with, "So a baby seal walks into a club . . . " and then I laugh and my mom is shaking her head and smiling and saying, "Oh, John *Lowell*. My high little boy," and I suddenly remember that I am high and that my mother is here and then there is a flood of information that drowns my brain in a heartbeat. I remember that I'm sick, that I have Cancer, that I'm only on the first round. I remember that I'm sterile. I remember that I might die.

I remember.

And it hits me like a bullet in the dick. I say, "Jade . . . " and she says, "Yes, dear?" and I say, "I have . . . cancer . . . " and tears well up in my eyes and she says, "Oh, geez, here we go." A salty tear runs down my cheek and I stick another Butterfinger in my mouth.

My mom makes pasta for dinner but I'm too full to eat, a sensation that has become quite foreign to me. Regardless, I sit at the table with my family instead of in My Yellow Chair and I have a discussion about faith and God and disease and purpose.

Now. Stop. Everybody put the brakes on. I don't know how to make a foot note in Word – I'm fancy like that – but would like to interject a side bar that is both, for me, equal parts ridiculous and necessary. Please bear with me for just one moment.

I was 26 when this cancer thing happened to me. I am 35 today. What? Yes. And in those 9 years God and I have developed a very strange kind of relationship. We're kind of like two kids that were dating in high school and thought they were going to get married and live happily ever after but then at the last moment one of us decided that the other one wasn't real and so that kind of threw everything about our relationship out of whack. You know how it goes. We don't really talk like we used to but I think about the old guy often and wonder what our world would have looked like if we'd stuck it out. But *that* is a story for another story.

There are some things coming up in this tale that felt true at the time and felt real at the time and how I personally align those two opposing world-view experiences is neither here nor there. This is not a story about religion and theology. That said, spirituality played a large part in my experience and so it must be included and it must be told and it must be represented as it was experienced at the time.

Disclaimer over. Please continue.

There is something about being on the very edge of life that forces you to walk directly up to the cliff and look over it. So maybe it's chemo-brain or maybe it's the sharp focus of death or maybe it's the evacuation of everyday routine like jobs and chores, but my world feels like it's falling apart—legitimately pulling away at the seams, the fabric of reality between this world and the next beginning to unravel.

I begin to feel a deep sense of calm connectedness to the world around me and to (what I would call at that time) God – a benevolent being. It's hard to validate emotional and spiritual experiences to other people because there is simply something inside every individual that happens and I can't make it more real than that.

For me, it was all real. It was experience. It was truth.

Every Sunday, regardless of how poor my health was, my wife, mother, and I would go to church. The music at the beginning of service would throttle my ears and penetrate my bones and make me feel as though my face were going to split open and snakes were going to poor out but it was a necessary evil to endure. Being there felt right and good and warm. There was a tangible hope that I could sink into.

Once the service was over, they would invite anyone who wanted prayer to come to the front. Strangers would place their hands on my shoulders and pray so fervently that I was certain their words were somehow more tangible than my own.

Once, during a particularly rough week when I was too tired to walk, my wife led a small group of individuals to the back where I was slouched in half, breathing deeply and wheezing. Four people I'd never met circled around me, this thing that looked like a pile of dirty laundry.

Among them was a tall red-headed woman whose regular Texan accent suddenly slipped sideways, mid-prayer, into a language I'd never heard as she began to speak in tongues. I'm not going to get into the theology of this and I'm neither going to validate nor excuse the practice. From the mundane to the bizarre, these are the events that occurred.

The tall red head, suddenly breaking back into English, speaks a single, penetrating phrase. She says, without knowledge of our infertility, "I see babies . . . lots and lots of babies . . . " and then it's all over.

So now, here at dinner, blitzed out of my gourd and talking to my mother about Christmas traditions and how Pagan celebrations were incorporated into Christianity, it is I who suggests creating chain links out of construction paper and draping them from the ceiling.

We created 147 loops, one for every day I had left in chemo, and on each loop we wrote a Bible verse and every night we'd tear one down and read it together. It was these evenings that I looked forward to the most—just sitting and thinking about one specific hopeful thought, allowing my weak and warbled brain to slowly digest it.

This chain would become my visual reference for the rest of my journey. If everything went according to plan, I could see the end.

And I could see that The End was still a ridiculously long way away.

*** *** *** *** ***

People ask me if I'm mad at God for giving me Cancer and I say that I don't believe He gave me Cancer any more than I think He gave me the flu or my buddy Ben the herpes.

Sorry, Ben. If you don't want to get your new shoes dirty, you shouldn't jump into a muddy hole.

We all have consequences for our actions, and even outside of cause and effect, I believe that we sometimes just draw wild cards. Perhaps this thing was happening to me because of personal decisions I had made—smoking, drinking alcohol, eating fast food, using microwaves—or maybe it was because of decisions my parents had made by not removing my distended testicle, or maybe it was family history and it was just an unavoidable fate that rested in my genes (my jeans), or maybe it was just my lucky day. I'd never really won any big raffles before and I suppose it was bound to happen eventually.

In any event, it didn't matter where it came from or who was to blame. It just mattered that I got through it, however possible. And for me, that meant clinging to God with everything my fried little brain and frail little body could muster.

CHAPTER 25
ROUND 2

There is a stop sign posted half a block from my house that, circa 10 days ago, I could barely walk to. With my mother holding me around the waist, the two of us feebly hobble down the sidewalk in order for me to get some of that Vitamin D and "exercise" that everyone seems to think is so important. By the time I touch the pole I am so winded and utterly exhausted that I'm ready to sleep. And I apologize for the redundancy, but I just really want to stress that I just walked 300 feet with the assistance of my mother and am now ready for a nap.

I am a side effect.

But that was ten days ago. Today I'm walking through a grocery store at 11 a.m. I'm still leaning a little heavily on the cart for support, but we've been meandering for fifteen minutes and I bet I've walked at least two thousand feet. Maybe even *three* thousand!

I can eat here and there without the assistance of the vaporizer and I can walk and I can exist in a world without vomiting because the chemo is slowly draining from my system and everything is getting better and sounds don't make my stomach churn and I'm starting to live again and . . . today I go back in for Round 2.

Today I start over.

There is a strange elation and excitement that fills my body and mind and maybe it's just hopeful naiveté but *I am excited to go back in.*

I've been receiving letters in the mail and phone calls and emails and messages via social media from various people—friends, family, friends of friends, friends of family, and even strangers who say they've been reading my blog and watching my story unfold and looking at the pictures my wife has been posting and they're just . . . *amazed* . . . at our fantastic attitudes.

"You're able to laugh at the whole thing!" they say and I, with tears streaming down my cheeks and quaking hands, think, *Har-har-har.*

But the letters and text messages keep coming. "My niece has cancer and I told her your story and sent her to your blog," and, "My son had cancer and God bless you," and, "Your story is so inspiring. You put my life into focus," and I sit in my chair reading these and feeling like a fake because of all my talk about death.

Last week I was in a state of true fear about my approaching second round. I couldn't dream of willingly going back and allowing them to do this to me, setting me back to square one. The needles, the poison, the nurses, the dark bags of chemicals dripping into me, the smells, the puking, the pain, the hunger, the fear, the fear, the fear and, most especially, The Unknown.

It's truly not the impending death that destroys you but the utter hopelessness of life, your energy being sapped and drained from your body until you feel like the last brittle leaf hanging onto a tree in an autumn storm.

Even chewing your food becomes a chore and a challenge because it takes too much of your scarce reserves. *But, Johnny*, you ask, *why don't you just get high all the time? If it helps your appetite and helps you sleep and gives you energy? Why aren't you getting baked? Go green!* And the answer to that, my little Doobie Brother, is because, while that little miracle drug works like a charm, it comes at a cost, an actual hard cost. I'm talking finances. And I can't just go on a binge and burn through every green dollar I own. For the next six months I have to buy groceries and pay rent, not to mention the myriad of other expenses that occur on a regular basis: car insurance, health insurance, electricity, etc., etc. May I remind you that I'm not working? We're rolling in a car with three wheels that's running on fumes and a prayer.

Watching our pennies disappear one by one, we call to inquire about government assistance but they tell us we don't qualify because we "made too much money last year." My wife says, "Yes, but last year my husband was healthy and had a good job. That makes sense. This year he has cancer and can barely walk and definitely can't hold a job and we need to eat," and the person on the phone says, "You will qualify next year," and my wife, says, "That doesn't make any sense," and the person says, "We rate you off the previous year," and my wife slams the phone onto the table.

I watch the clock tick tock away and think that every second I'm just a little closer to The End, whatever result it may be, life or death. However this fight turns out, we're chugging full steam ahead.

Two hours till go time and I feel positive. I try to soak everything in because I know that my happy moments are limited and finite. I know that tomorrow morning I'm going to be lying in bed with my eyes slammed shut, feeling sorry for myself. I know that tomorrow there will be nothing but pain and hunger. Gotta get sick to get better.

So today, now, in this moment, I just soak it in, trying to take pictures of everything in my mind, storing it all away to look at later. How does the air smell? How do the birds sound? How does this food taste?

Chemo ruins everything. It manipulates your taste buds, turns your eyes to delicate glass orbs and your ears to amplifiers. Everything is blinding and gluttonous excessiveness. Every piece of stimuli feels like a flood hitting your brain and drowning it. It feels like everything is coming in but nothing is going out and your skull becomes crowded with blurring and buzzing. Chemo covers your brain in moss and turns all your memories and thoughts into fuzzy bubbles and television static. Life becomes a copy of a copy of a copy; details falling away, edges blurring, clarity collapsing.

Courage is not the absence of fear, but the triumph over it (and yes, I read that on a poster in a doctor's office). And, this *Courage* with a capital C that I have acquired quickly becomes *courage* all lowercased once we pull into the parking lot and I'm left staring at the monolithic hospital that will become my home for the next five days. I stare at it, my prison, trying to keep my composure steady, my attitude high.

My wife says, "Look here," and I turn around and she snaps another photo of me entering the hospital. I look considerably thinner in this one; my beard gone, my cheeks a little deeper, my eyes red and dry around the sockets.

We enter the building and my courage sinks down and vanishes. I squeeze my hands into fists and think, *I don't want to be here I don't want to be here I need to get out of here*, but I keep walking, into the elevators, onto the fifth floor, down the hallway, into my private room, my spa, my cell.

I lay out all my personal accouterments (journal, pen, iPod, Bible) and sit on the bed. Jade finds the show about the family with all the kids and now I guess they're having another one. I ask her to change it. The show about the man losing his face is on again and we decide to rewatch it.

The nurse enters with the IV while I stare at the TV, thinking about the wilderness and camping. She sticks me and walks away and that's it. I'm now tied up to the stables like one of the horses in a sad western. Me and my pole, buddies for life.

Suddenly, the machine I'm connected to starts beeping and a small Asian nurse in her early fifties rushes in, presses a few buttons, and straightens out my tubes. She says, "Hello. My name is Sue. I will be your nurse for the next couple days. You are . . . Johnny." I smile and wave my hand. She says, "How are you doing?" and I say, "Well, all things considered . . . " and she says, "Yes. You have very bad cancer but we are going to *fix you*! You are *young* and *strong* and you have *good blood* and *good veins* and *good attitude*!" and my wife says, "Sometimes . . . " and Sue laughs and she lights up the room and she says, "We no allow bad attitude here! You take it somewhere else! Here—only good attitude! Because we fix you! I be right back!"

And she turns to leave and I say to Jade, "I like her." Sue returns with my first bag of chemotherapy and a small piece of chocolate, which she gives to me. "You feel well? You no have chemo for two weeks?" and I say, "Yes. That's right," and she says, "You eat this now before you get sick!"

I open the chocolate bar and she flips a switch and here . . . we . . . go . . . .

*** *** *** *** ***

Hours later, I wake up all alone in the middle of the night. My room is dark and quiet save for the incessant beeping that is coming from my IV machine. I shift my body weight and examine it to see if there's some giant red warning button I can push.

Nothing.

I navigate my hand down the side of the bed and find the CALL NURSE button. A few moments later, a pale chick who looks like she's been working the nightshift for too long wanders in and asks what's wrong. I tell her I don't know. I tell her my IV thing is beeping. She hits a quick combination of buttons and everything goes silent. I ask, "Why does it do that?" and she says, "Means there are bubbles stuck in the tube," and I say, "Bubbles? Won't those kill me if they get in my veins?" and she says, "Yeah . . . . . they can," and then she turns and leaves without saying anything else.

I lie in the dark and stare at the shut blinds, wishing I could see the stars but knowing that, even if they were open, LA's blanket of smog would cloud them from my vision. I think about my wife and mother, both sound asleep in beds forty minutes away. My wife has to work in the morning so I'm flying solo tonight. We toyed with the idea of my mother staying behind but ultimately decided that the hospital bed just wasn't big enough for the both of us, even with her curled up at the bottom like so many teacup Chihuahuas.

In the hallway, I can hear various machines and hospital mechanics at work in the silent hours. Beep. Beep. Beep. A heart monitor. I hear a machine that sounds like it's breathing for someone. *Kerrrrr*—inhale. *Vhoooosh*—exhale. Underneath is a man moaning, his wails creeping down the hallway like fog. It is the groaning of a man lost in delirium.

I shut my eyes for a moment and when I open them, an old man is standing in my room with a plastic briefcase. He pulls out a syringe and takes my blood. I shut my eyes and when I open them again, a young Latino gentleman is standing in my room emptying my trash can. I shut my eyes and when I open them again, a young African American woman is standing in my room with my breakfast. I tell her I'm not very—gag—hungry and would she please mind taking it away but leaving the orange juice, which I casually sip on.

I stare at the clock and watch its arms turn. I stare at the window and watch the shadow of the sun rise. I listen to footsteps in the hallway pass. I try to catch conversations but nothing sticks. I wonder who else is on this floor: old people, young people, someone I could talk to, relate to, converse with?

I hate the doctors telling me what I'll feel, how I'll feel, what to prepare for, what to expect. They only know because they've been told. They don't *know*. They have no personal point of reference. This is one of the loneliest factors—surrounded by people, you feel alone in your experience.

My mother arrives; my wife arrives. I curl into a ball and shut my eyes. It's happening again: never-ending motion sickness. I put my hands over my face and breathe deeply. Jade asks how I'm feeling, and instead of answering, I just shake my head, trying to fight back The Great and Hopeless Depression that is rising up inside of me, threatening to take over, The Voice that whispers inside my head, "Every day. Every day. Every day you'll be sick. I'm never leaving you. You're trapped here, stuck here, and every day those nurses are going to enter and keep filling you with Sickness, more and more, and just when you think it's over, you'll be back and you'll do it again. You think today is bad? Think about tomorrow. Think about the next day. Think about next week and the week after that and the month after that and the month after that. This road you're on is a long one, Johnny, and I'm going to ride your shit into the ground. You think today is bad? You have no idea. You have no idea what I'm going to do to you. You have no idea how long this will go," and, because I no longer have any grasp on time and because my minutes stretch on for days, this really could be some relative millennia.

Anxiety begins to twist a knot in my guts as I try to understand the overwhelming process that lies before me and the pain I have to endure before this is all over. My mom asks if I've eaten breakfast and I shake my head again, hands still over eyes. My mom asks if I need to "medicate," and it takes me a moment to grasp what she's asking me. I nod my head and slowly sit up, the movements sending my equilibrium reeling. I can feel my brain sloshing around inside my skull like dirty water in a fish tank.

My mother sets a small suitcase on my bed and unzips it, pulls up the cover and begins digging through various articles of clothing, bathroom paraphernalia, and pill bottles, pulling them out one by one. Then I see it. Sitting at the very bottom of the suitcase is my vaporizer. I chuckle thinking about my mom smuggling, what basically amounts to a very fancy pipe and soft drugs into a hospital for me to smoke. Do I want to "medicate"? It's the closest thing my mom will ever say to, "Honey, do you want to get baked?"

But, I suppose this is what it's for. This is how we should be treating it. If *medicinal* marijuana is to be used and respected as an actual drug and if it actually wants to shake it's street stigma, then perhaps I should be *medicating* and not *getting high*.

Jade helps me stand up and leads me into the bathroom. I lean against the wall and slouch to the floor. My mother hands me the vaporizer and, while I try to find a proper place to set it, she plugs it into a nearby socket. My wife hands me a small box that contains various strains of *medication*, as well as my grinder.

My mother turns to leave and my wife holds her hand out to me and says, "Here. I made this for you." I reach out and take a toilet paper roll stuffed with scented dryer sheets. She says, "It's a filter . . . to hide the smell." I say, "You're Bill Nye!" and she says, "You're Tommy Chong." I smile and she shuts the door.

The bathroom is silent save for the quiet murmur of the television creeping under the door. I open a pill bottle, select a "pill," grind it up, place it in the bowl, heat it up, and pull.

We have take off.

The anxiety in my stomach loosens, loosens, loosens, disappears. I begin tapping my finger to some Beatles song that pops into my head. My depression vanishes. I hold the homemade filter to my mouth and blow through it. Everything smells like Mountain Spring Grass.

I pick up a comedy book about ninjas called *Real Ultimate Power* written by a man posing as a child named Robert Hamburger. To this day, it's one of the funniest books I've ever read, stoned or sober. I laugh so hard my sides hurt. I laugh so hard that I cough. I laugh so hard, I can't breathe.

In the other room, I hear a nurse enter. Sue. I hear my wife say that I'm in the bathroom. I hear the nurse ask if I'm having a *bowel movement*. I hear Jade lie and say, "Yes." I hear the nurse say she'll be back.

Jade knocks on the door and says, "Hurry up in there, White Snoop Dogg! They're looking for you!" and I say, "I'll be here for five days. They'll find me," and I laugh and take another hit and then I say, "Just relax, White Marge Simpson."

Robert Hamburger talks about how he saw a ninja cut off a man's head once just for dropping a spoon in a restaurant and then I stare at an illustration of a samurai for 15 minutes. The artistry of the drawing is astounding.

In the other room, I hear Sue return and ask where I am. I hear Jade say that I'm still in the bathroom. I hear Sue ask if I'm constipated. I hear my mother say something about, "Just being a man, taking his time." I hear Sue say she'll be back. I hear Sue leave. I hear Jade bang on the door, louder this time and far more aggressively. She says, "Hey, Jerry Garcia. Get your ass out here! You've been taking a shit for 35 minutes, and it's starting to look suspicious."

"OK, OK," I mumble and slowly clean all my paraphernalia up, tucking it behind the shower curtain. I crawl to the toilet, using it to brace myself while standing up and then slowly walk out of the

212

bathroom with the biggest, dopiest expression my face can muster. As I open the door, I try to hide it, not wanting my mom to think I'm . . . what? Wait . . . high . . . ? She knows. There's no reason to hide it. Is this OK? What is happening? I think I've done something wrong.

My mom says, "Take your time," and my wife says, "You know how uncomfortable it is to lie to them? They're freaking out because they think you're constipated. You do that again and I'm telling them you need an enema."

Just as she finishes her thought, Sue walks back in with her cart and says, "Johnny! You are here! You are all right?"

And I say, "Yes! Great!"

And she says, "You poop OK?"

And I say, "Far as I know!"

And she says, "You in bathroom long time. You no strain?"

And I say, "No. Just reading a book,"

And she says, "OK. You tell me you constipated. I get you more pills,"

And I say, "OK."

She tells me she needs to take my vitals and I say, "Cool,"

And she says, "You want to sit down?"

And I say, "Can I stand?"

And she says, "You . . . can . . . if you have the energy,"

And I snap my fingers and say, "Sweetheart, you better believe it."

She sticks a thermometer in my mouth and I say, "How's it look?"

And she says, "You're alive. That's good,"

And I say, "No doubt. Hey, thanks for giving it to me orally. The guy last night gave me an anal exam and it was really painful." Jade says, "*JOHN*," and my mom says, "*Ew*," and Sue says, "What was his name?" and I say, "I don't know but he just kept breathing really heavily in my ear."

Sue wraps a cuff around my bicep to take my blood pressure and I casually glance around, overly aware that my heart seems to be beating weirdly slow. Buh-dunce . . . buh-dunce . . . beating to the rhythm of a Pink Floyd song. She presses a button and I feel the band tightening on my skin, squeezing it like a really weak boa constrictor and then slowly, slowly, releasing. Sue looks at the digital read out and says,

"Huh," and I say, "What?" and she says, "Your blood pressure is a little low," and I laugh and my wife quickly interjects with another half-cooked lie. "Yeah, it's always a little low. He's just a very chill fellow, he-he . . . " and Sue says, "Hmm . . . " and I shrug and say, "Sue, listen. *Listen*. I feel good. I feel great. You wanna see me try to moonwalk?" and she says, "Nope. I'll be back later. You strong. Good attitude."

Over the course of the next few days, Sue becomes a fourth member of our group, sitting on the end of my bed and hanging out to chat after she takes my vitals. She hangs around my room even when she's off duty and pokes in before going home just to make sure the night nurse has everything under control.

In the mornings she brings me muffins, and even though I can't eat them, I am grateful for the simple gesture. In the afternoon, she comes to me and says, "Nurses have big feast downstairs. Pot luck. I bring you food," and then, sure enough, forty minutes later she shows up with nothing less than eight plates of home-cooked goodies ranging from pastas to banana bread to casseroles to desserts hailing from various homelands; Germany and Holland and Spain.

She tells us about her past life—where she grew up, what her parents did, how long she's lived in Arcadia. She tells us she loves to cook and says she'll bring us some "real Korean food" after catching us eating Panda Express for the third day in a row.

Twenty-four hours later, she appears with a menagerie of hot plates and store-bought chocolates that the four of us share in a communal setting.

Cancer is a very lonely disease to have because most people you know simply fade into the background. It's a disease that makes people uncomfortable. They don't know what to do or what to say or how to respond or what to bring you. Nobody is showing up to sign your cast and I believe it's just too depressing to come visit your friend or family member while they slowly turn into dried fruit. Here you are, stuck in a bed, a needle shoved in your arm, looking like a pretty accurate living depiction of a mummified Egyptian Pharaoh, which is to say, decrepit and dusty. Your friends enter and they see you as you are, not as you were, and they see you trapped here in this hospital, in your cute little nightgown and they know you'll lie here for six days and they feel bad for leaving. They feel like they have to stay or they're abandoning you. They feel guilty going back to their lives while their friend molds and becomes one with the hospital bed in holy union. It's easier . . . to just not show up. Things are safer at a distance.

And for the person with cancer—for me, for you, for your cousin or aunt, for the person sitting in the chair or the bed, for the person getting the chemo drip-dropped into their veins like a toxic tributary—this act is beyond infuriating.

It is heartbreaking.

During the Apollo 8 missions, astronauts Borman, Lovell, and Anders would lose contact with Earth for forty-five minutes as they disappeared behind the far side of the moon during each of their ten orbits. Some may say it's the loneliest anyone has ever been, being completely out of touch with your own species.

The radios were dead. Contact was dead. The three of them were in complete and utter isolation, blocked off from the entire human race. Granted, Earth was still there and Earth still carried on and the Earth people still went to work and smiled and laughed but somewhere in the darkness, three men sailed quietly and desperately through the solitude just hoping to come out the other side, hoping to reestablish contact, hoping to, eventually, be integrated back into humanity after they'd viewed it from such a new and exhilarating perspective.

Ideally, I don't have to spell out my analogy for you because I think it's fairly spot on. Also, P.S.: In my parallel, I am Frank Borman because he is straight up dreamy. My mother and wife can fight over the other two in our made-up, playtime scenario.

Your family members who you've grown up with and your friends who you've shared your life with, people who would stand up with you in a fight, back down against cancer. Nearly everyone leaves you alone, fragmented, isolated, and blocked off from the world. People stop calling. People stop writing. People stop coming by. Even before you're gone, you don't exist. You're the dead and dying dog at the shelter. You're the starving kid in Africa. You're the homeless family on the street, and you are easier to ignore.

Your sickness, your issue, your *thing* you're going through is so bizarre and weird and awful and outside the realm of possible imaginings that people just slowly vanish into the crowd, and while you sit alone, grasping at any hope, you think about them and you wonder what they're doing and you wonder why they're not calling or writing or coming by. You wonder what you possibly could have meant to them. It saddens you, it angers you, and it breaks you. It makes you feel like an old and forgotten toy left out in the rain.

And I say this not as a self-pitying statement (although I am aware that it is how it sounds), I say this as a warning. If someone you know has cancer and if you've made yourself scarce, you have abandoned a person of your tribe during his or her greatest need.

I get it. It's hard to be involved. It's hard to step up to the plate and put someone else's needs before our own. It's hard to be selfless, and it doesn't come natural to any of us. We're humans and we want things to be easy, but we're *humans* and we're in this together. And maybe the awful truth of cancer wouldn't feel so foreign to us if we all stepped onto the altar and looked into the coffin; if we all took a chance and said, "I'm here for you because you need me to be." When you watch from a distance, everything is filtered through the lens of a camera. It's difficult to get your hands dirty when you just paid for a manicure.

But Sue . . . Sue was born to have dirty hands. Her short-cut nails spoke of a baker who had her fingers in many pies. She cared with the true compassion of a parent. She wasn't merely doing a *job*. She was living her life and making sure it was worth something.

I think about Sue often, and though I've never written her a letter, I've sat down to do it on several occasions but am always stopped by some voice asking if she would remember me, another Face in the Crowd. She had a significant impact, not only on my cancer journey and experience, but also on my healing process and my point of view on life. How can I be more like Sue? How can I help those around me? How can I give what I have—my heart and soul and identity—how can I pour that into something to show someone love and compassion?

There are people that try to make the world a better place. Budda. Jesus. Bono. Sue. We are all capable if we try.

CHAPTER 26
TAKE CONTROL

You know that feeling when you've got the flu and your stomach is just rolling around in your guts? That feeling where the back of your throat feels sensitive? That feeling where you just shut your eyes and cover your mouth and try to take some slow and easy breaths, telling yourself, "Just relax. Don't puke . . . " but no matter what you say you *know* that you're going to eventually lose it and you're going to have to make a mad dash for the bathroom and hopefully, hopefully, *hopefully* you're lucky enough to actually make it to the toilet before your lunch bursts from your cheeks like a fire hose?

That feeling? You know the one. That's how chemo makes you feel all day long.

Somebody says, "You need to eat something! Want a bite of salmon?" and you just shake your head and wish they'd stop talking about fish.

You know that feeling when you haven't eaten anything all day and you're so hungry that you're actually considering feasting on really weird foods that you typically wouldn't touch? You're like, "Oh, if I only had a cheese-covered pretzel right now! If I only had a meatball sandwich with black olives and mayonnaise! If I only had a taco pizza that was folded in half into the shape of an actual taco . . . . "

That feeling when you're just starving and ravenous and you don't want to eat, you simply want to consume . . . . That's how chemo makes you feel all day long. Because you can't eat. Because you throw everything up. So you're constantly starving.

Two feelings that exist on completely opposite ends of the spectrum come together in your body and cause the perfect storm. It's loving and hating someone. It's giggling and crying. It's jumping and falling.

This is chemotherapy's intermission Round 2.

I'm sitting back in My Yellow Chair wishing that the doctors would just put me in a drug induced coma for the next few months, loss of time be damned.

One of our friends comes over. It's easier to meet us at our house, on a level playing field, than it is in my hospital room, which is truly one floor above a morgue. She's pregnant and stays for dinner. My wife and mother talk to her about the baby and her boyfriend and their life and their plans and their names and how excited they all are. Meanwhile, I sit in My Yellow Chair, eyes closed, breathing slowly and willing myself to not puke in front of our guest.

For dinner, I gorge myself on 12 grains of rice and half a baby carrot.

I slowly stand up, casually excusing myself. My wife and mother both rise, "Do you need help? Are you OK?" but I wave them off, smile and mumble, "Just fine." (Breathe deeply). "Be right—" (breathe deeply) "back . . . " and then I disappear around the corner, into the bathroom, and shut the door behind me.

I drop to my knees, grab the toilet seat, stick my face six inches above the water and puke, once, twice, three times. I lie my face on the cold porcelain and try to remember a time before this; when my biggest concern was being punctual for work. I heave again and more stomach bile rises up in my throat. I hate what I've become. This is not who I am. I'm supposed to be sitting at that table, telling jokes and making people laugh and I'm supposed to have my legs crossed with one arm thrown tightly around my wife but instead I'm a dying animal, hunched over the toilet with my face stuffed into a receptacle for human waste.

My lips are dry and my throat is parched, an ancient tube filled with desert sand. All I want is water to pour down onto me, into me, through me. I want to feel the cold refreshing waves rush over my tongue and down my gullet, filling my belly with icy relief until I can hear the liquid sloshing inside of me. But I know that if I drink, if I swallow, if I even open my mouth, I'll be sick. I know that any water I drink comes back up and I know that the process is painful. I know what I want and I know that I can't have it and then I'm trying to stand up, clutching the edge of the sink. I'm pulling myself up, saying, "To hell with the pain," and my weak knees are shaking and I punch the faucet and the water is pouring down and I know it's going to hurt so bad but I just need something to ease my constant thirst and then I thrust my face under the falling water and chills run down my spine and I'm taking in huge gulps, barely stopping to breathe. I gasp and shut my eyes and drink more and my stomach is expanding and stretching and crying out for me to stop but the water tastes so good and I want to scream and cry and I want to drink more and so I do. It's rushing down my cheeks, down my chin, soaking the collar of my shirt and I'm swallowing and coughing and swallowing again and I know I'm about to regret this.

I lie my head on the counter and just listen to the water run out of the faucet and down the drain, the sound one of the most peaceful things I've ever heard. My hand fumbles around and finds the handle, brings it down and everything is silent. My legs give out and I drop back to the ground, palms down. I breathe heavy, trying to relive the immediate relief of the cold water but only feeling the hurt coming on and my gorge rising. My stomach is crying out in pain and I don't care. This is the price I pay.

I throw myself at the toilet and a fountain of water bursts from my mouth with such force that I'm sure my cheeks are gyrating under the sheer magnitude. Every splash, every drop, every ounce comes rushing out and I feel it all—the perfect negative of all the goodness I'd previously ingested.

I tip over sideways and wipe my mouth on my sleeve. Someone knocks on the door and Jade asks if I'm all right. I mumble something and she goes away.

My stomach starts to cramp and I roll over, facedown, curling into a tight ball on the floor. I turn my head and see dust bunnies under the sink. So many dust bunnies. They're reproducing. I rest my face against the frigid tile floor and try to push the chill through the rest of my body, which suddenly feels on fire.

Breathe . . . slowly . . . *gag* . . . breathe . . . slowly . . . *gag* . . . *gag* . . . . I sit up, bend over the toilet again and vomit up more creamy acid that, instead of being yellow, is pink in color. My stomach contracts and I vomit again. Bile that is not pink but red. My stomach contracts and I vomit again. Bile that is not red but crimson. Bile that is not bile but blood.

I stare at the pink droplets branching out in the water like a family tree and wonder where it's coming from, why it's coming from my mouth, my stomach, ulcers . . . definitely could be. Definitely could be caused from stress. Could the lining of my stomach be torn from vomiting so much? So harshly? Makes sense. It could definitely be that. Could it be stomach cancer? Giant tumors growing in my belly, eating away at my innards, making me rot from the inside out? No. It most definitely couldn't be that. It's most definitely not that thing. It's probably one of the first two that I mentioned . . . the, uh . . . the ulcers or the ripped stomach lining. I decide to just let that be what it is and assume that my body will simply repair itself in the following days.

Do I *want* to go see a doctor about this? Absolutely not. Do I think that I probably should? Logic is a wild beast when dealing with matters of the heart. One can make oneself believe nearly anything if the event calls for it. Persuasion, to an audience of yourself, is astoundingly simple. I say, "Of course you don't *want* to go to a doctor . . . because there is no need. They would make much to do about nothing and you have, if nothing else, *this* under control.

I have this under control.

This thing, this thing that belongs to me, this bit of knowledge, is mine and mine alone and it is something that I can hold in my hand and look at and decide what will become of it. When I'm in a hospital bed being wheeled up and down hallways and shoved into machines and having drugs pumped into me and having my lungs tested and my vitals taken and my blood drawn, it's all out of control. Nothing is mine; not even I am mine. But this . . . this is mine.

What has become of me? How did I get here? This is me understanding that I have lost total control. This is me bent over a toilet filled with my blood. This is me, completely helpless to my inner maladies and my outer surroundings.

This is what Cancer looks like.

In the other room, I hear our friend packing up to leave and someone knocks on the door again and Jade says, "Angie is leaving, do you want to come out and say goodbye?" and I just say, "Uh . . . I . . . can't," and Jade says, "I'll give her your best," before I hear her footsteps disappearing down the hall.

I puke again and, looking down into the toilet, I realize that there is so much blood resting in the bowl that if I had stumbled upon this horrific scene unknowingly, I would assume that one of those I-didn't-know-I-was-pregnant girls had decided to drop calf in my house.

A few hours later, another friend, Jake, arrives just to say hi. My mother opens the door and says, "My . . . you look just like Jason Bateman," and, truly, Jake does. I say, "*Teen Wolf 2*," and Jake, probably too stoned to function, just smiles at me, having not seen me for quite some months. The change that has taken place in my face has been gradual, sneaking up on me the way holiday weight does; but to Jake, who last saw me fifty pounds heavier, is visibly shocked at my physical appearance. He stares at me and says, "There are two black holes where your eyes should be." I nod and pat the couch. He sits down and my mom begins asking questions about Jason Bateman's recent resurgence into the public's eye. She talks about his career in the '80s and about his sister, "His sister, what was her name? She was on Family Ties, I believe. Sarah? Samantha? Jennifer? Jennifer Bateman?" and then she turns to

Jake and asks, "What is her name?" and she says it with such genuine interest that I think she must have forgotten that this is not Jason Bateman nor is this fellow in any real relation to Jason Bateman, nor does he have any idea who Jason Bateman is outside of his roles on *Arrested Development* and, of course, the aforementioned *Teen Wolf 2*.

My mother says, "He got arrested? For what?" and I say, "No, it's . . . a show . . . . It's . . . " and she says, "On TV?" and I say, "Yes. A show . . . on TV," and she says, "Is his sister on it, too?" and I say, "I . . .don't think so," and she says, "Was this back in the '80s?" and I say, "Yes . . . it was in the '80s. He and his sister Samantha Bateman starred in it," and she says, "Huh . . . I'll have to check this out on IMBD Database dot com," and I say, "I-M-D . . . nevermind."

And then Jake leaves and then I throw up more blood and something inside of me says that maybe I shouldn't be hiding this and so I casually wobble into the dining room, supporting myself against walls and counters like a wino on a bender, sit down next to Jade and say, "Jade?" and she says, "Oh, geez. What? What is it now? What have you done? What is happening?" and I say, "Wh-what? Wh-what do you mean?" but my inflections are all wrong so I sound really guilty.

I say, "I just threw up," and she says, "What's new?" and I say, "It was bloody . . . I mean . . . . It *was* blood. I just threw up blood. From my mouth."

228

Jade stares at me but says nothing. She slowly sets down her pencil and slides her Sudoku puzzle away from her. She stands up and walks to the closet while I say, "I think it's fine. I think it's just a stomach—" gag "thing and it'll probably—" gag, "take care of itself but—" gag, "I just wanted you to—" gag, "know."

Jade slips on a coat and I say, "You going to the store? You going to pick up some Pepto-Bismol? You mind grabbing a Butterfinger while you're there?" and she says, "We're going to the hospital. To the E.R. Now," and I say, "Hey, uh, wait now. What's that?" and she says, "You're vomiting up blood. *BLOOD*. You're throwing up blood. Do you look at that scenario and think that's normal?" and I say, "Well . . . " and she says, "SHUT UP. You've got cancer of the almost everything and now you're throwing up blood. I'm not taking chances. You're," and I try to interject but she says, "NO. Whatever you're going to say. No. Just put on your sweater and your jacket and your hoodie and your overcoat and your scarf and your hat and your mittens and let's go," and like a scolded puppy, I stick my tail between my legs and do as I'm told.

On the way to the hospital, my mother sits shotgun while I sit in the backseat thinking that *everything* is out of my control. Stupid secret. Should have just kept it all to myself. Should have just let my stupid stomach heal all on its own. Two or three days, I bet that's all I'd need.

We pull into the parking lot and I manage to walk into the E.R. by myself. A young male nurse approaches and leads us into the back, sets me on a table and tells me that a doctor will be with us shortly.

Various people come through this long and narrow room that we've been put in—more of a hallway with beds, curtains, and various machines than an actual room. I lie down on the thin bed and breathe slowly, not wanting to vomit again because it hurts so badly. The contractions rack my body with pain and cramping and my skin breaks out in sweat and then chills and I can feel the stress and strain all the way down in my toes.

I shut my eyes and think about how I wouldn't even be here if I'd just kept my big, dumb mouth shut and not said a damned word. Jade says, "Are you OK?" and I say, "No," a black mood rising up inside me that's very ugly. I don't want to be here and I don't want to hear what some stupid doctor has to say and I don't want another IV and I don't want to be lying on this cold, hard excuse for a bed and I don't want to be around all these sick people with my already compromised immune system and I don't want to keep throwing up and I don't want to wait one more minute for this incompetent physician to walk through the curtain because *this is the EMERGENCY ROOM AND JUST WHAT IS THE HOLD UP*?!

Sometimes being mad at something is the only control you have. More often than not it's the *wrong* thing to do, but like a secret that's been told, once it's out there, it can never come back.

I tap my foot on the ground and Jade says, "Relax," and I say, "I shouldn't even—*we* shouldn't even be here. This is a waste of time and money. *Time and money!*" and Jade says, "Relax," and, "Smile," and she takes another photo of me.

I say, "How do I look?" and she says, "Really horrible," and I say, "Then you probably got my good side." The curtain shifts around and a young doctor who appears to be too young to be a doctor enters and sits down and says, "OK, so what are we dealing with here today?" and I say nothing because I already know how this works. I sit here and play the garden gnome role—silent and stupid looking—while my wife dishes all the details. She says, "He has this and that and he's sick with this and that and we've been here and there and they've told us this and that and here's this paperwork and these cards and this information and then a few hours ago he started throwing up blood," and the doctor looks at me and says, "How much?" and Jade looks at me and my mom looks at me and I say, "Just a little," and Jade says, "*How much*?" and I say, "I don't know, like . . . a quarter size every time I puke," and the doctor says, "And how often do you vomit?" and I say, "All the time," and he says, "And what color is it?" and I say, "The blood . . . is red . . . " and I cross my legs and my arms. *Take. THAT!*

231

Doogie Howser presses the tips of his fingers together just below his nose before saying, "OK. We're going to need to do a rectal exam," and both of my eyebrows rise into the air and I don't need to hear one more word because I am stepping into this situation and *taking control. THIS* will not be taken away from me. My butthole is MINE. I say, "No, we won't," and now it is the doctor's turn to raise his eyebrows and lower his hands and he is clearly not used to a patient in the E.R. telling him what will and will not be done. He says, "Excuse me?" and I say, "We won't be doing a rectal anything," and Jade says, "John . . . " and I firmly say, "*No.*"

Jade sees that this has gone beyond basic stubbornness into the realm of the untamable and so turns to the doctor and says, "What is it for? The rectal exam?" and the doctor says, "We need to see what color the blood is, if it's pink or red or black. If it's black, it's very bad," and I say, "It's red. Bright. Red," and the doctor says, "We need to do a test to see what color the blood is. The rectal exam gives us the closest—" and I say, "It's bright red. It's not black. You cut your finger. Blood comes out. It looks like that," and the doctor, ignoring me, says, "It's really just a quick procedure," and I say, "Are you listening to me?" and the doctor says, "It's very brief, just a quick culture and—" I say, "I'm going to be sick, hand me—" gag— "something. Quick," and the doctor grabs a kidney shaped bedpan and hands it to Jade who hands it to me. I lift it up to my mouth and puke up a sizable chunk of *red* blood, stand up, walk

232

over to the doctor, hold it under his face and say, "Is that a good specimen?"

The doctor looks at me and says, "That's red blood. You probably just tore your stomach from vomiting too hard. I doubt it's ulcers but we'll give you some medicine anyway. I'd like to keep you overnight just to make sure. Is that OK?" and I say, "No," and Jade says, "John . . . " and, this just being stubbornness now and not actual decisiveness, I say, "Fine."

CHAPTER 27
CHRISTMAS EVE

If the fifth floor of the hospital was a kind of relative paradise for chemo in-patients—big rooms, big beds, remote controls, specialty nurses—then the second floor was one step above a skid row methadone clinic.

A red-haired nurse who's seen better days leads us out of the elevator and down a narrow hallway with, I kid you not, a flickering fluorescent light. The tiles in the hallway are cracked and breaking, green and white checkered, garbage cans are over flowing and puddles of water seem to be leaking out from the cracks in the walls. We pass a clock and I see that it's just breaking 2:15 a.m. and is officially Christmas Eve.

My eyelids are getting heavy and my legs are feeling even heavier. I'm running on fumes, and when they lead me into the dark room, no one even bothers turning on a light. I lie down in bed, my wife covers me up, says something about coming back later, my eyes flicker, and she's gone.

I wake up forty-five minutes later, lean over the side of the bed and puke into the garbage can, unsure of where the bathroom is. The cable connecting me to my IV, which they gave me in the E.R., cramps up and starts beeping. Nobody comes. I press the CALL button on my receiver but nobody comes. I press it again… and again . . . and again . . . but nobody comes. BEEP-BEEP-BEEP.

The thought of bubbles traveling down the tube into my veins doesn't bother me so much as the actual noise of the blips. Each tone acts like an arrow through my skull. BEEP-BEEP-BEEP. It holds open my eyelids, slides a metal plate under my eyeball, shoves down, pops it out, disconnects my optic nerve with a hacksaw, and jams a white hot screwdriver into my brain.

I reach out into the darkness and push the machine as far away as I can, 3 or 4 feet. I push the CALL button again . . . and again . . . and again. Ten minutes pass. Fifteen minutes pass. Twenty minutes pass. I look around and see a phone just out of my reach but don't know whom I'd actually ring.

Suddenly, in the hallway, I hear footsteps approaching. A shadow begins to grace my narrow vision through the doorframe. Finally. Finally. *Finally*.

A nurse with dark skin and purple scrubs approaches . . . and continues on . . . heading somewhere else. I cough into my hand and shout, "HEY! EXCUSE ME! UH . . . MISS?!" The footsteps stop and I hear the soles of her shoes turn on the tile before they begin to grow louder again. She turns into the room and, seeming unsure, says, "Hi, how are you?" and I say, "This machine, it's . . . I don't know what's—" gag— "wrong with it and—" gag— "can I get some nausea medication? I'm—" gag— "I have cancer and I—" gag— "sorry . . . I just need something for my stomach and I don't think this call button works," and the nurse says, "I'll see what I can do about the medication. Your call button should work fine. I'll get you some ice chips," and she turns to leave just as I lose control of my stomach and vomit more blood into the trashcan.

Twenty minutes later a man enters and takes my blood. I puke again. I roll onto my side. I mash my face into the pillow. I turn on my other side. I can't sleep. The sloshing sickness in my stomach is listlessly rolling through my entire body. My brain feels like it's bleeding. My toenails hurt. My bones hurt. I try to sleep but am wide awake, alone, cold. Where is my medicine? I start to gag again and my stomach feels like someone is twisting a knife into it. I slam my thumb into the CALL button three times in a row before shouting, "HELLO?!" Nothing.

Another man enters and says he needs to take my blood. I tell him someone was just here forty minutes ago. He says he doesn't know about that even though I show him the Band-Aid and the hole. He takes blood from my other arm. I tell him I need a nurse and he says he'll fetch someone. Twenty minutes later the nurse shows back up. It's 3-something-a.m. at this point and I feel as though I'm about to begin hallucinating with exhaustion. I ask about my nausea medicine and she says that she spoke to the pharmacy and they said I'd need a doctor's prescription first.

This is how hospitals work. You have stage 4 cancer. You're skin and bones. You're a grown man who weighs 130 pounds. You've been admitted to the E.R. for vomiting up blood. You have a track record of various ailments and, at 3:30 in the morning, nobody will give you medicine to stop you from throwing up *more* blood because the doctor, who is asleep, can't sign off on a form.

The nurse, in all of her wisdom, brings me enough aspirin to tame a mild headache. This is tantamount to trying to fix the World Trade Center with Elmer's Glue. I would kick her in the teeth if only I had the energy. She tells me she's trying to get a hold of the physician and I say, "Isn't he asleep?" and she says, "Yes but . . . uh . . . we're trying to reach him . . . " and I say, "OK . . . please hurry." The nausea is growing in me like a weed, choking out my life and energy, taking over all my thoughts.

The Useless Nurse leaves and the machine starts to beep again and the first man enters and takes my blood again, claiming that he didn't get enough vials for all the tests. I tell him that a second man was already here and that he should have quite enough between the two of them and he tells me he doesn't know of a second man. He pokes me in my arm, takes more vials and leaves, fetching the nurse. She returns, adjusts the machine and says that there's still no word from the doctor.

It's 4:30. I sit up in bed and stare at my feet, thinking about how I'm not even halfway through this process yet. Wondering if this is how death looks. Wondering if these will be my final memories. Not *this moment exactly* . . . but a collection of moments just like it—hospitals, nurses, beeping, cleaning solution, needles, blood, vomit, and stiff hospital sheets, crunchy with starch and dried urine. I puke again and the blood seems to be retreating, being replaced by yellow bile. *That's a good sign*, I think to myself. I lie back down, place my forearm over my face, and try to force myself to cry. It sounds lame but sometimes a good cry is all you need.

Instead of crying, I puke again. My stomach is a war zone filled with corpses.

I stand up and make my way to the dark bathroom, the fluid from the IV bag washing through me and cleansing my kidneys from all the poison I've taken in. I am a junkie, drugs coursing through my veins, ruining my life.

I pee, crawl back into bed, and watch the sky start to turn gray. The clock reads 5:45 and I still haven't slept. Still no word from the pharmacy. Still no aspirin or ice chips. This place is getting a bad Yelp review fer sher.

At 6:15, the second man enters my room again and says he needs to draw my blood. He says they had enough blood but forgot to do one test. Beaten, broken, destroyed, I say nothing. I just stick out my thrice-stabbed arms and let him take as much as he wants. I turn on my side, pull my knees to my chest and wonder where my wife is, where my mother is, where Sue is.

I press the call button. Nothing.

At 7 a.m. the Useless Nurse shows up with more Aspirin. I swallow it and puke it up. She says she's still waiting to hear from the doctor. I don't say anything. She leaves.

At 8:50 my wife shows up and I am so happy and hopeless and helpless that I finally do cry. I am so alone without her. I tell her everything and she says, "What? WHAT? *WHAT*?" and when the first man enters to take my blood *a fourth time* because someone just called in one more test, Jade says, "No. You're not taking his blood. Get out. Get out of here," and the man says, "But we—"and Jade says, "That's too bad. I'm sure you'll figure something out. Leave." And the man turns and walks away.

The Useless Nurse enters, and before she can speak, Jade says, "He needs his nausea medication," and the nurse says, "I know, he—" and Jade says, "No. You *don't* know. He's in here because he's puking up blood and you give him, sorry, *aspirin? ASPIRIN?* Where did you go to school? His call button doesn't work? Where are we? What is this place? You think *ice chips* are going to help him? He can't eat. Did you call the doctor?" and the nurse says, "I . . . left him a message . . . " and Jade says,

240

"Where's the pharmacy? I'll go talk to them," and, twenty minutes later, my wife, not an employee of the medical field, returns with good news. She says that someone will bring me a bag right away—not a pill, but a bag of medication so I can't throw it up.

At 10:15 a.m. we ask if we can go and we're told that the doctor wants to see us first. At 11:30, we ask where the doctor is and they say he's making his rounds but will definitely be here before noon. At 12:45 we ask how much longer he'll be, and they say he's on his lunch break but will absolutely probably be here directly after that at some point. At 1:15 Jade leaves to get herself lunch. At 2:30, he still hasn't shown up but somebody tells us that he's on the fifth floor. At 3:45 people stop showing up to our room. At 4:15, there is still no sign of anyone. At 5:15, a male nurse walks by in the hallway and my wife grabs him and says, "Where is Dr. Manfred?" and the nurse says, "He should be here shortly," and Jade says, "Can we leave whenever we want?" and the nurse says, "Yes . . . I mean . . . we can't force you to stay but . . . a doctor should see you," and Jade says, "You have 15 minutes to bring him here or we're walking out this door." At 5:30 Dr. Manfred shows up sporting an arm cast and says to me, "How you feeling?" I say, "Good." He says, "Throwing up blood?" I say, "No. Not since last night." He says, "Good. Call us if anything changes. You may leave."

This is how hospitals work. Well-oiled machines of idiocy.

CHAPTER 28
ALAN

I haven't eaten anything of true substance for months—just bites of candy bars, portions of cereal, some chicken, rice, carrots. I can eat when I'm high, but I can't always be high. I've lost over one quarter of my body weight. The man staring out of the mirror is not me. It's not JOHNNY. It's some dark replacement, a temporary placeholder.

When I was in high school, a kid I was supposed to graduate with died of bone cancer during our senior year. I only knew him by proximity, our entire graduating class consisting of about 300 kids, but found myself attending his funeral regardless. When somebody that young dies in a town that small, it sends a ripple through the community that everyone feels.

I remember standing in front of his coffin and staring down at him. The boy, his name was Alan, would never be called *big*. In his Earthly life he was never going to be a successful football player and he didn't have the physique for track. He was a gear head with a very average-sized body. Nothing particularly large or small about him but that was not who I was looking at in the coffin. Average Alan was not staring back at me. This body was a shadow of his existence. His skin looked jaundiced, his cheeks were hollow bulbs, his head appeared to have grown in size, pulling his hair line back although I understood that it was all smoke and mirrors, death's way of manipulating your perspective. His head wasn't growing; his body was shrinking, or rather, had shrunk. His fat cells had been depleted.

Some mortician's assistant had painted him and tried to give him blush and color and *joie de vivre* but . . . he was just a dead kid with make-up on. This wasn't Alan. This was just Alan's body, and his killer was hunting me.

Now, almost a decade later, I see Alan staring back at me in the mirror. The pasty skin. The bland features. The inhuman persona. I would look more at home in a George Romero film.

Is this what I'll look like when I die? Is this what people will see? Will remember? Is this who my wife will recall? This sad little man hunched over in a chair, spending his days sleeping?

I picture the people I've seen at nursing homes, men in recliners staring at birds in cages. Old men staring, watching, waiting for the end. These men who were once vigorous young boys, running, jumping, dancing, chasing, fighting, kicking, screaming, laughing, living. This is what time does. Eighty years, ninety years, one hundred years. Time saps away everything precious and leaves you with the remains. It eats all the food and gives you the wrapper and hands you the bill.

This is me, a ninety-year-old man watching birds, just glad to finally be out of that hospital and back in the safety of familiar surroundings. Me, sitting in my backyard with a blanket across my lap, my eyes shut, listening to that distant chirp, chirp, chirp.

When this journey began, sitting outside to get Vitamin D was a joke, some kind of pathetic attempt to grasp at straws. Today I'll do anything to try and get better. I'll do anything for a bit of strength. I'll take your magic pills. I'll swallow your magic beans. Somebody tells me that raspberries help cure cancer so I buy a palette full of them and try to eat a few every day.

I haven't heard anything about my cancer markers in some time and have no idea what they're doing; 300, 600, 14,000, 62. It doesn't matter. I feel like shit. I shut my eyes and listen to *chirp, chirp, chirp* and it's just so beautiful. The birds are so calm and soothing. I watch a small brown one jump from branch to branch. *Chirp, chirp.* I watch a squirrel run up a tree. I watch a row of ants marching back and forth, back and forth, back and forth at my feet. Somebody walks through my alley and I wonder where he's heading. The guy looks at me and wave and say, "*MERRY CHRISTMAS!*" even though it isn't until tomorrow. I raise my hand halfway up, too tired to speak. This is what Cancer looks like. Saying "Hello" feels like a quick run. Saying "Merry Christmas!" with all of its syllables and uppercase letters and its great, big, tall exclamation point is a marathon.

I inhale deeply, hold the breath, count to five, and then slowly let it out. In the house to my left it sounds like someone is showering. In the house to my right it sounds like someone just broke a dish. In the tree 20 feet in front of me I hear a bird chirping and think about how I am the only one hearing this noise; this little bird is singing its song while the world goes to work and pays bills and buys clothes and sleeps and watches reality TV and here I am, sitting in my backyard all alone, the sole audience for the performance of a lifetime.

I feel as though I am able to examine the world around me in great and fascinating detail. I feel like I am seeing it in a fourth dimension. I feel like the strands of existence are breaking and tearing and opening up and I'm able to see through them into some other realm of beauty. I'm seeing things that no one else can. I'm seeing the color green for what it is. I'm seeing *green grass* and it's so beautiful and I understand that it's so beautiful and everything I've taken for granted, the wonderful, majestic world around me, is suddenly alive and vibrant and vivacious. The trees are towering monoliths, hundreds of years old. The dirt, the grass, the bugs, everything is working together in perfect unison, perfect harmony, a world separate in my very own backyard.

I look at it all happening and I see everything. I see every detail. I hear everything. I see how intricately everything works together. I see the ants. I see a bug eat an ant. I see a bug get stuck in a spider web. I see the spider eat the bug. I see a fly. I see a piece of disgusting dog shit and I see the fly land on it and plant maggots in it and everything, everything, everything, even the most disgusting, grotesque pieces of us play a greater role. It's perfect, it's flawless, a complicated tapestry of interwoven threads. When I die I'll feed something, fertilize the earth, turn into a tree, give oxygen to everyone.

Perfect.

I turn my eyes inward and stare into my body and see my lungs and my heart and my lymph nodes turning black. I see the disease fighting to survive. I try to understand what it's doing, what it's thinking, what its purpose is. Maybe it's supposed to cull the herd. Natural selection.

I stand up and go back inside. It's Christmas Eve 2008. I slowly walk through the house and shut all the blinds, sit down in My Yellow Chair and stare at our Christmas tree, glowing white and red.

My mother had told my wife she shouldn't worry about the tree. She tells her there is so much on her plate. She tells her to just relax. But my wife says no. She says she's going to put it up. She says we're going to celebrate Christmas. She says we're going to be as normal as possible. This is her grasping at her own sense of control in an otherwise chaotic existence. The two of them put up the tree while I watch. That was four weeks ago. Tonight I just soak in its radiance. I want to crawl underneath it and stare up at its electric stars, drowning out the world around me in color and design.

Instead I walk to my bedroom and lie down, pull my stocking hat over my face, pull my hood over my head, pull my blankets up to my chin and try to sleep but instead just stare at the back of my eyelids, breathing heavily, trying not to vomit.

In the other room I can hear my mother and wife rolling dice for yet another game of *Yahtzee*. The sound of the cubes hitting the table is like hammers pounding steel. Their voices are like forks scraping against glass plates. Everything feels like hot wax being poured over my brain. I cover my ears with a pillow and squeeze. I can hear them making dinner, something with pasta in it. The smell reaches me and I furl into my hobbit hole even further, deeper. I want to go somewhere else, be somewhere else, be someone else. I want someone to take my place, to deal with these effects. I want to walk away.

Jade enters and says, "Dinner's ready," and I fall out of bed, onto the floor and pull myself into the kitchen. The delicious aroma of manicotti makes me gag and I say, "Smells great." Truly, I want nothing more than for someone to take that whole pan of disgusting shit tomato pasta and throw it out the window. I sit down at the table and casually cover my mouth and nose with my hand. My mom asks if I'd like just a little and I shake my head and take a sip of water. I shut my eyes and listen to these two women, my closest family, my caretakers, the one, the woman

248

who brought me into this world and the other, the woman who will be by my side until one of us goes out, talk about recipes and marriage and cleaning.

Halfway through dinner I get up and go back to bed and lie down and sleep.

I wake up just after midnight. It's Christmas.

CHAPTER 29
CHRISTMAS

It's a beautiful, traditional, California Christmas morning, which is to say, it's an even 60 degrees with no snow in sight. I open my eyes and my wife says, "Merry," and I say, "Christmas, dear," and she kisses me and I wonder how long it's been since we've had sex. The thought of not "being physical" for the next three months makes me feel just as ill as the thought of actually attempting to.

Jade rolls out of bed and I stand up, hunched over, and we both walk into the living room where my mother is making coffee. She's always up before us, dressed and ready to go with her day. She says, "MERRY CHRISTMAS, ONE AND ALL!" and I say, "Merry Christmas, Mother! I wonder what Santa brought me!" and then I look in my stocking and, already knowing that it's completely empty I say, "Damn you, Santa! I'm not dead yet!" and my mom says, "John *Lowell* . . . " and my wife says, "What do you want to do for breakfast?" And I say, "This morning . . . you know what we need to do?" and both women look at me and I say, "We need to do something really special. We need to make sure we remember this breakfast. We need to make sure that we never forget it," and they both lean in and I say, "Mick . . . Donald's . . . pancakes," and smiles spread across both their faces and my wife says, "I can be persuaded to eat McDonald's pancakes!" and my mother says, "Now we're talking," and I say, "With butter," and my mother says, "And syrup!" and my wife says, "And those weird hash-brown cakes!" and I say, "You can have mine!" and my wife says, "SCORE!" and then she runs out the door and I rub my hands together, trying to decide my next course of action.

My mother says, "Honey . . . " and I say, "Si, Madre?" and she says, "Do you need to . . . medicate?" and I say, "You betchya, I do!" and so my mother goes and gets my box filled with herbal supplements and she sits down at the table next to me and I watch her grind up various nugs and place them in the vaporizer. By the time Jade returns with the food I'm so full of energy and vigor that I meet her at the door, bow down very low and say, "Welcome, back, m'lady! How goes your sojourn?" and she says, "Food-food-food," and we lay the plastic trays out on the table and I say, "I'm so excited, I'm so excited, I'm so excited right now."

We open each tray and slather gobs of butter between the hotcakes and dump rivers of hot maple syrup all over the fluffy stacks and I tear in with my fork and start shoving piece after piece into my mouth, imagining my body putting on fat just as quickly as I'm losing it. I force down, three, four, five bites in a row and shout, "*It's so good*!" and the three of us *clink* our pancake bites together and then I'm snapping and moon walking again.

This is Christmas morning 2008.

I will never forget it.

CHAPTER 30
LOCKJAW

It is an easy life to wake up every morning and to hate our jobs. It is an easy life to piss and moan while we drive to work. It is an easy life to hate our bosses and to begrudgingly accomplish a list of tasks set out before us. It is an easy life to be put upon, allowing the world and circumstances and fate to blow us this way or that way and to kick the ground and say, "If only my luck would change."

It's easy to be a victim.

Whether it's a bad marriage or a job that is uninspiring or a disease that catches us off guard, it's easy to slouch down, shut our eyes, and feel sorry for ourselves.

It is also very amazing how quickly our perspective will shift and change once these horrible responsibilities that have been "placed on our shoulders" are suddenly gone and missing. How desperately we would eat the scraps from the table we were previously dining at.

Sitting in My Yellow Chair, I think to myself that I would do near anything to have my job back. To have *any* job back. I would go back to the video store I worked at as a senior in high school, I would go back to the coffee shop I worked at as a junior, I would go back to the sandwich shop I worked at as a sophomore. Paperboy, garbage man, toll-booth attendant, just let me live. Let me stand in the sunshine and talk to someone. Let my cares be menial and pointless and let me eat turkey sandwiches for lunch. Let me leave at five and drive home in bumper to bumper traffic and give me my thoughts—reasonable, logical thoughts. Let me think of my wife as the woman I married and love dearly; let her be the object of my affection and desire and let me not see her as my caretaker any longer. Let me grow old and come to take care of my mother. Don't let my mother stand by idly and watch me die, cradling her son in her arms as I shrivel away, fading further and further into The Black.

Give me Life. Give me Freedom. Give me Adventure. I want to sail. I want to scuba dive. I want to scream. I want to skydive. I want to camp, hike, and swim. I want to travel in an RV. I want to visit Nicaragua and Ireland. I want to live in the woods. I want to fire a gun. I want to make a movie. I want to write a book. I want to have a family, grow old, and die with no regrets. I want to learn to play guitar, cook, and perform sleight of hand magic tricks. I want to stand up in front of a large group of people and say, "*THIS* is my story. *THIS* is what happened to me. *THIS* is how I got through it." I want to donate my time to something, someone, anyone. I want to donate my money to something, someone, anyone. I want to make a difference. I want to talk to a child with cancer and say, "You're going to be OK." I want to alter and inspire those around me. I want to effect change. When I die, I don't want to say, "I wish I . . .

"Instead I want to say, "I did all." If I saw it, I took it. Life is a fruit tree and everything is waiting to be picked and gobbled up. Some fruit is higher than others but, with the proper motivation to climb, all is attainable.

All is attainable.

More than anything, though, when I come out the other side of this disease, and you believe me, mark my words, I will—when I come out the other side, I am going to be a different person. Baptized by fire, existence will not look down on me but I will look down on existence, and I will conquer it and I will own it and I will eat everything it has to offer.

When I can walk, I will run. When I can think, I will write. When I can move, I will create, accomplish, execute.

Until then . . . until then, I will sit here and I will hibernate and I will simply try to inspire myself.

Cancer has a very vicious duality to it. The one side, the first side, the more prominent side, is very sad and dark and depressing. It's very aggressive. It has sharp teeth and it bites and it (literally) kills you and (figuratively) those around you. It attacks your mind, body and spirit. It chips away at you piece by piece and makes you hate yourself and your life and your existence. But then, there, on the obverse side, is the stranger side of Cancer; the bit that people rarely speak about and the bit that the public rarely sees. Cancer is inspiring and life changing. It will clear your mind. The world comes into focus. The path becomes clear; the path of movement and forward momentum; the plan of attack.

My mother looks at me and says, "What are you thinking about?" and I look up and say, "I just want to live," and she says, "I know . . . you will," and I say, "No . . . I mean . . . when this is over. I want to go—" I reach up and touch my jaw. Something feels Wrong. Off. Stiff.

I place my thumb under my jawbone and apply pressure and I rub my cheek and I try to open my mouth but suddenly my teeth are clamping down on each other with the tenacity of a bear trap and my mom says, "What are you doing?" and between pursed lips I say, "I . . . can't open my mouth."

And so, how do you respond to that? Someone has a seizure, call 911. Someone is turning yellow, put them in the sun. Your heart hurts? You're probably having a heart attack. Your face is going limp? You're the victim of a stroke. These are obvious decisions but . . . I just can't open my mouth. My mom says, "Does it hurt?" and I say, "Uh . . . no," and then we both sit in silence trying to figure out what to do in the least dramatic scene of all time.

I wave my mom over and lift up my hands and she grabs me and I stand up and I say, "Let's go for a walk," and, instead of going outside, we just manipulate ourselves in a great big circle around and

258

around and around the inside of my house. I make seven laps before I'm completely winded and need to take a break.

In the kitchen, I lean heavily on the counter, stick my fingers between my teeth, and try to pry my mouth open. It's a scene directly out of a *Tom and Jerry* cartoon. Jade enters and says, "What are you doing?" and I say, "I can't open my mouth," and Jade says, "Why?" and I say, "I don't know. I think I have lockjaw," and Jade says, "Right . . . " and I say, "Look at me! My jaw . . . is locked! I cannot open it! I have no key! How much more evidence do you need?!" and she steps forward and examines my face and says, "Hmmm. We could take you to the doctor?" and I say, "NO! No more doctors! No more IVs! No more hospital beds until I have to go back for the chemo. We're figuring this out on our own. Who do we know? Can we Ask Jeeves?" and all of my words are coming out in chunky gusts and gasps.

My mom says, "Your aunt used to be a nurse," and I say, "Yes! Absolutely! That's right. Get her on the phone. Let's solve this mystery!" and now my teeth are biting so hard into each other that it actually is starting to hurt and I'm getting so tired from standing up that I decide to go lie down on the couch, burying my face deep down into the crevices of the pillows.

I hear the phone click and my mom says, "Drink milk," and I say, "And then what?" and she says, "I don't know. I guess that's it. Something about . . . blood and . . . I don't know."

Jade raises an eyebrow and shrugs and says, "You should probably get more calcium in your diet anyway," and I say, "But of course," and she pours me a tiny glass and I drink half of it, gag, drink the other half and sit down. Jade brings me another glass and I sip on it before, slowly, like oil on the Tin Woodman in Oz, my joints begin to loosen and I can stretch my jaw and talk again.

Cancer is, if nothing else, a very tragic adventure unlike any other that I've been on. Like a haunted house, it keeps you on your toes and it keeps you guessing and it makes you roll with the punches. *Seizure*! Swerve, block. *Blood transfusion*! Uppercut! *Heart cancer, lung cancer*! Pop-bang! "And now here comes his signature move: *Lockjaw*!"

Of all the things Cancer is, boring is not one of them.

I shut my eyes and wonder what tomorrow will bring.

CHAPTER 31
SOLAR ECLIPSE

Once in a *great* while the sun and the moon align in a total solar eclipse and the stars uncross and the fates smile and, like a miracle from the hand of a savior, I am able to stand and to walk on my very own. I am able to laugh and tell jokes and drink juice and taste food without getting sick.

These are not the days when sickness is almost out of my body. These are the days when the cure almost is.

On the days when the chemo is nearly out-processed and I am beginning to get my thoughts back in order and the soft mush that is my brain is beginning to firm up, it is these two or three days before going back to the hospital that I must take advantage of my circumstances.

As my wife helps me bundle up in my full arctic wear, complete with scarf, I notice that the clock reads 6:15 p.m. I know we need, need, *need* to be home by 9 o'clock at the very absolute latest because, no matter how good I currently feel (relatively speaking), I won't make it to 9:15 p.m. Quarter after rolls around and I will, home or not, be dead to the world. My carriage will turn back into a pumpkin and my clarity will turn back to pay-per-view static. Goodbye, world. *Au revoir. Adios.* Time to sleep.

Jade unlocks the car and I fall into the passenger seat and turn the radio on, letting music quietly fill the air.

I miss it so much. Of all the superficial things, I miss music the most. I can hear the raspy voices of Kurt Cobain, Frank Black, and Isaac Brock coughing out lyrics in my furthest memories, but it's like listening to them through a joint wall shared by a neighbor in a duplex.

Bad news comes, don't you worry
Even when it lands
Good news will work its way to all them plans

Jade cranks the key, slams the gear shift, and punches the gas and then we're off like a herd of turtles, gently coasting down the streets of The Valley, navigating through streets with powerful names like Victory, beautiful names like Magnolia, and disgusting names like Cumpston. We pull onto the freeway and the night envelops us, pulling our automobile into her black cloak and then, at 80 miles per hour, a song by Rage Against the Machine begins to *wah-wah* out of the radio and Zack de la Rocha's voice suddenly reminds me of how this all started; me blasting through the desert to Vegas, alone, hungry for drugs and alcohol. Me with a couple hundred bucks on fire in my pocket. Me with my invincible bullshit attitude and . . . I hate that guy. It's only been three months but I don't recognize him and I can no longer relate.

The things that guy wants are moot. His desires are dead. I don't feel remorseful or sorry. I don't mourn his loss but secretly celebrate it, wondering who this new skin will shape up to be once it gets to crawl out and spread its wings. How will his brain think? How will his heart feel? What will his soul search for?

Only time will tell but tonight his soul searches for Mexican food in the flavor of a little *restaurante* in Westwood. Some friends of ours had called us a few weeks back, requesting a dinner date and my wife tells them, "Yes! Perfect! We'd love to see you!" and they had said, "How's 7:30?" and Jade had answered with, "Perfect. How is nineteen days from now? Johnny should be in some kind of working order by then."

The silence on the other end of the phone lasts for a few moments before my friend's wife says, "I'll have to check the calendar . . . yes? Maybe?" I have nothing to do and no time to do it in. My life is a blank page that I can't read. My days are newspaper articles written in Cantonese. My nights are like iPods with no headphones. I am existing without being operational. Here I am, flesh and blood, present in time and space, but unable to be useful.

Jade pulls into the parking lot, gives the keys to the valet, and we both walk inside, she dressed up for a well-deserved night out, me looking like a homeless man trying to pass for "merely unemployed." None of my clothes fit as I'm in the

263

exact opposite stage that most pregnant women find themselves—too big to fit into their old clothes and just too depressed to go buy more because they know this season will be over soon and they can squeeze back into those old jeans and T-shirts.

In the meantime I look like that Fievel Mousekewitz character from *An American Tale*, oversized rags hanging from my body.

This is our first outing since The Beginning. This is the first time we've been out of the house to somewhere that was not directly related to Cancer: hospital, clinic, marijuana dispensary, church. It's also the first night that my wife and I have been away from my mother since she got here and it somehow feels like our little circle has been broken and one of our members is absent from a meeting.

We enter the warm building and find our friends, Killian and Emily, sitting on a small bench in the "Just Have a Seat" area. They approach and hug us, both of them dwarfing me, wrapping their average sized arms around my depleting frame and crushing the life from my bones. They say, "How are you?" and they say, "You look good," and they say, "This place is our favorite," and they say, "You really do look good . . . " and I know that I look like an emaciated version of The Yellow Bastard from the popular graphic novel, *Sin City*.

The waiter points us to our table and we walk through the cramped spaces, navigating to our booth in a back corner. We sit down and I try to take it all in. I want to remember this. I know my time is almost up. The eclipse is almost over. My chariot will be a pumpkin before too long.

Strange hand-painted tribal masks hang along the walls the entire length of the restaurant—blue faces with white lips, orange faces with blue dots on the cheeks, black faces with red streaks running from the eyes, one hundred vacant expressions watching us from the walls.

I'm staring into one of these masks, getting lost in thought when I realize that a *senorita* is standing by my side taking drink orders. Like clockwork, all three guests—Killian, Emily, and Jade—order extra large margaritas. I smile. Even Jade is taking advantage of her own solar eclipse.

The waitress looks at me and says, "Margarita for you, sir?" and the thought of consuming salty alcohol makes me shiver. I say, "No, thank you. I'll just have the, uh . . . " and then I glance back at the menu, run my finger down their alcohol menu, stop on a random drink, look back up and say, "Milk, please," and the waitress stares at me and says, "Milk. Like . . . a White Russian?" and I say, "No . . . like, two percent," and Jade laughs because she knows it's the only thing besides Gatorade that's actually able to help soothe my stomach and sore throat. Killian says, "You can get a margarita. Dinner's on us!" and I laugh and say, "Milk is fine. Thanks."

Back around the table again, the waitress takes our meal orders. Killian gets a number 17 combination plate of four shrimp tacos, beans, rice, two enchiladas, and a side salad. Emily orders a number 4: smothered chicken burrito with a bowl of tortilla soup on the side and an appetizer of jalapeño poppers. Jade orders a number 11: two chicken enchiladas, two beef enchiladas, rice, beans, and two sides of her choice for which she requests double portions of corn cake. The waitress turns to me and I put down the menu, my mouth slavering from all the options and I say, "I would like . . . a taco, please," and she says, "A taco meal?" and I say, "A . . . sorry. I would like one taco," and then, just to add a little cultural flair I say, "Uno. Taco. Por favor." And I know she doesn't understand why I'm ordering so scarcely and I don't feel like explaining the whole long story or even some shortened and bastardized version of the tale that goes something like, "I'm sick and tonight is my night to eat a delicious meal and I'm very excited but still, I'm sick and I can't eat like a totally normal person. I still have to be aware and conscious because I am completely aware and totally conscious that I puke every single day, multiple times a day, and I am also aware and conscious that I am in a public establishment with my friends and family right now, a public establishment that is filled mostly with strangers, and I don't want to vomit here. I don't want to vomit on your table. I don't want to vomit on your floor. I don't want to vomit in front of my friends, next to their food, ruining their meals. I haven't eaten much in the last few months and so my stomach has shrunk down to a fraction of its previous size. No longer a softball, it's now a walnut." Killian says, "You can order more. Dinner's on us!" and I say, "One taco is all I need."

I imagine taking them up on their offer and ordering a "regular portion" for the sake of being polite. I imagine it arriving, the plate overflowing with food, steaming with flavor, the waitress saying, "Careful, it's hot," as she sets it down on our table with pot holders. I imagine everyone grabbing their forks and digging in, ravaging their food, tearing apart those gummy enchilada rolls, shoveling refried beans into their mouths and slicing chicken and beef like butchers while I stare at my plate and eat half a taco before sliding the plate up and saying, "So good . . . so full . . . . "

The waitress leaves and our pre-dinner conversation starts and I quickly realize just how out of the game I've been. They ask us if we've seen this show or that show and they ask us if we've seen this movie or that movie and they ask us if we've heard this news story or that news story and Jade reaches over, under the table, and squeezes my hand twice, gently, in a friendly manner and I know she's thinking the same thing I am, which is, "I have no idea what is going on in the world."

We've been so ingrained in our adventure, so zipped up in the body bag that is Cancer Life that the rest of the world has slowly passed us by. While we've been huddled around the fire, trying to stay warm, Wall Street has continued on, Hollywood has continued on, Earth has continued spinning and changing and growing.

The words that everyone speaks float from their mouths to my ears but die before they ever hit my brain. Everything feels superficial. Everything feels plastic and fake. Not my friends, not my wife, but our words. Hollywood and Wall Street. It all suddenly feels so . . . dirty. Everything feels so fleeting. When life and death are hanging in the balance, money quickly loses its value because you realize it can't help you. It can't buy you health. It can buy you healthy food and it can buy you good doctors but it can't buy you health. Health, like respect, is earned.

A moment later a young man appears at our table holding a tray of drinks, a young man who is decidedly *not* the young woman who had originally taken our orders and so he is unsure exactly which margarita goes to which patron. He says, "Straw . . . berry?" and Emily raises her hand and he sets it down and says, "There you go . . . . Mango?" and Killian says, "Right here," and reaches out and takes it from him and the waiter says, "Passion fruit?" and he looks at Jade and me and Jade smiles and says, "I'll be taking that," and then all of our eyes are resting on his tray where the only cup left is a tiny half-sized little sippy cup with a Styrofoam lid and a wacky bendy straw and the guy says, "Sorry, I . . . I thought this was for a kid," and I say, "Yeah, that's right. You *better* go put my drink in a big-boy glass."

That night, on our drive home, I can feel the effects of our night out. My eyes are heavy, my arms are anchors, the weight of one taco pulling me down and drawing me into darkness. I fall asleep on the ride home and when I wake up I'm in my bed. The eclipse is over. The carriage is gone. Tomorrow it all starts over again.

Tomorrow is Round 3.

CHAPTER 32
ROUND 3

I'm sitting in the backseat of our Pontiac Vibe in the parking lot of the Arcadia Methodist hospital. My breaths are coming in quick staccato bursts, my heart threatening to beat right through my rib cage. My mother is sitting in the passenger seat saying, "Just relax. We're in no rush . . . just calm down," and my wife is saying nothing, knowing that there is nothing to say. She sits in the driver's seat biting her nails and checking her Facebook, knowing that I just need to process these emotions myself.

I throw myself back onto the seat and say, *"I'm not going. I can't go back in there! I . . . . Please, GOD, don't make me go back in,"* and then I'm curling my knees into my chest and covering my eyes with the bend of my elbow and just begging for a miraculous healing because I am terrified of chemotherapy.

It is burning and damaging and destructive. It is fire and earthquakes and hurricanes. I am a witch being led to the pyre again and again and again. I'm walking over hot coals, walking into the pain willingly, tirelessly, for the third time. It was easier when I didn't know. It was scarier when I didn't know but it was easier. The unknown was untouched territory that I slowly felt through in the dark, finding the rhythms of my sickness, the pulse of my body, the schedule of my Sub Life.

271

Now I know. Now I'm aware. I see the guillotine and the hangman's noose. I see myself curled over and hurling up blood in less than 24 hours. I see my bones feeling like glass. I see my stomach churning and rolling as paint thinner is pumped into me. The fire is lit and everyone is chanting, "C'mon, c'mon, c'mon . . . round three," and I say, "*It's not even the end! It's not even the end . . .*" and images of doing this entire thing *one more time* keep flashing through my head and I'm so scared and I'm so alone and I don't want to get out of the car. I just want to die, to die, to be struck dead. I am Prometheus and my liver is eaten and renewed and eaten and renewed and eaten and it doesn't end, it never ends. *God, if you won't heal me, kill me!* I am begging for a miracle, either of fantastic goodness or diabolical madness, anything that will deviate me from my current course of action.

I can taste the saline they pump through my veins to flush my IV. I can smell the cleaning supplies. I can hear that beeping IV ringing in my ear, stabbing my brain. I can hear that machine in the hall breathing for the man who is either still alive or very dead. I can feel the needles resting in my arms, and my eyes are glass and my ears are bleeding and everything stinks, physically stinks of rot and death and body odor.

Jade shuts her phone off and says, "Johnny," and I say, "Hhhhh," and she says, "We need to go inside now," and I stand up and hold her hand and she takes another picture of me outside of the hospital,

272

paper thin and red eyed and then we're walking inside
and you already know how this plays out.

CHAPTER 33
MINOR DETAILS

In the hospital, over the course of the following week, I get sick, I sleep and I listen to people talk. Everything happens as I imagine/predicted/knew. The Cure consumes me and turns me into a writhing mop of hopelessness.

The back of my throat is sore and bleeding, completely unrelated to Cancer and chemo, just a side effect of having no immune system. My wisdom tooth on my right side begins to force its way through my gums, making my jaw line feel swollen. Every time I move my mouth, a needle gets shoved into the root of my tooth. I drink Anbesol by the liter, hoping to drown out the pain.

I sit in the bathroom, get high, blow it into our homemade prison filter, apply Anbesol and try to eat, but everything is just too out of control. The Cycle is in full force and nothing can slow it down. There are no breaks on this ride.

Marijuana and over-the-counter pain medication aside, I still have a tremendously sore throat that feels like it's made up of aluminum foil. Eating has become this thing that I used to be able to do; I am a bird with clipped wings dreaming of flying.

Dietary calls me and asks if I'd like the chicken or fish and I know they both look like they've just been pulled out of a drain pipe so I say, "Could I just have six iced teas, please?" and the man says, "Excuse me?" and I say, "Iced tea. You have iced tea?" and he says, "Oh . . . yes," and I say, "I don't want any food. You may keep the food. But I would like six glasses of your iced tea. It's very delicious," and he says, "Uh, yes. Yes, OK . . . six . . . uh . . . iced teas. Anything else?" and I say, "Popsicles," and he hangs up.

While we wait for lunch, my mother and I slowly walk downstairs, IV in tow, outside to the "garden area," a small block of concrete with a fake tree in a wicker basket. We sit on a bench and let the sunshine touch our skin and I notice, even in the middle of the day, even in the daylight, everything is cast in blue. Everything is cold and sterile. Everything is prosthetic. Half a block away, standing by the street, I see a healthy-looking man smoking a cigarette. My heart breaks for him and my guts wrench in my stomach and I want to run to him and say, "Listen to me! Look at me! I have lung cancer! Put that thing down! You're young! You're beautiful! Go get married! Go buy a fast car! Go to a rock and roll show!" and I want to rip the cigarette out of his mouth and stomp on it and just wheeze at him.

Instead I just gag and my mom asks me if I want to head upstairs. From the garden to our room on the fifth floor, it's an easy four-minute walk, moving at a nice casual pace; the kind of pace where you put your hands behind your back and whistle.

It takes us twenty-five minutes. If I moved any slower I'd start drifting backward through time. I take small shuttling steps like a slow-motion Geisha, one floor, one hall, one tile at a time. We reach the elevator and my mom presses the CALL button while I sit down on a nearby chair, trying to catch my breath for the second half of our epic quest, this adventure from the garden to the room that is nothing short of Frodo's quest to Mordor; my will and fortitude, my stamina and strength being tested.

The elevator door slides opens and a mother walks out with a young boy, maybe eight or nine. He's got straight blonde hair the color of notebook paper and dull brown eyes, his shirt sporting some superhero television icon of the week. He's healthy. His mom is healthy. I see their visitor badges and know that they're either on their way out or on their way to the gift shop to buy candy bars and dying flowers.

Suddenly, I have this moment of clarity and I am standing outside of time and space. I'm shot through a wormhole and I can see this kid who's standing in front of me, barely old enough to be called a prepubescent. I see him growing up. I see him meeting a girl and falling in love. I see that the girl smokes and I see that he takes one of her cigarettes. I see them driving down the freeway. He smokes two back to back and his buzz turns to nausea. I see him turn 18 and I see him buy his first pack. I see his summer fling with Chesterfields, his love affair with Parliaments and his eventual marriage to Camel Lights. I see him standing outside of a hospital on a blue day, smoking a cigarette while some kid with cancer watches him from a hundred yards away, wishing there was something he could do to stop it, to show him, to intervene.

The kid walks past my mother, my pole, and myself and looks up at my skeletal face, my yellow skin and my dead eyes. I say, "Hey," and he and his mother both stop and she turns and looks at me but I never break my gaze with the kid. I say, "I've got lung cancer because I smoked cigarettes. Don't ever try them, no matter what, because you might end up here like me."

And then I reach out and press the 5 button and the kid and the mom just stare at me as the door closes, both of them looking caught off guard, their mouths cracked ajar. To this day I don't know if it was a good idea or not. I don't know if it did anything or had any effect, but I hope it planted a seed.

Back in my room the six iced teas have already been delivered and are positioned perfectly 3x2 on a large plastic tray. I sit down on the bed, insert a straw, and pull a few drops into my mouth, tilt my head back and the plan is to let them trickle down my throat painlessly but my reflexes kick in at the last second and my Adam's apple rises and falls and I'm forced to swallow and the pain sears the back of my throat like a cattle prod and I grimace and shut my eyes.

When I open them a man is standing in my room with a plastic briefcase and I know what he wants even before he asks but I don't want to give it to him and I kick and scream and they restrain me with physical force and leather belts. They strap me to the bed and I try to bite them and I spit at them and curse. A large black man shoves his ass onto my face while a smaller white man grabs my wrist and commands my wife and mother to hold me down while he takes my blood. I scream and cry through the black man's butt but it all comes out in noises that sound like a tuba. *Grrr! Raaah! Blluuu!* He jams the steel into my flesh and pulls out my blood and I bite the black man and he forces my head sideways and I try to bite his fingers and my wife is crying and screaming and my mother has mascara running down her face and she is wrenching her hands and they've both dropped to their knees, embarrassed at my less than civilized behavior and then the men are gone and I'm left panting, drooling, foaming at the mouth spitting out, *"You don't know me! You don't know me! Don't judge me! You ain't been where I been! Walk in my shoes! Walk in myyyyyy shoes!"*

Granted, this exchange is all allegory but will hopefully give you a greater glimpse into my psyche, a peek into my internal emotional breakdown, a preview to how I feel when those needles come out. The emotions tend to run high. Things become exaggerated . . . .

Days pass and nights pass and reality TV shows come and go and begin and end and nurses come and go and I get high and sober and I vomit and try to brush my teeth and vomit again. My wife and mother come and go, arriving in the morning and leaving in the evening. I stare at the ceiling and at the tiles and at the blank, black, dead television, and the television looks back into my blank, black, dead eyes. I turn it on and watch an episode of *I Love Lucy* with the sound completely muted. Even with no one talking I can tell where the jokes go, where the audience is supposed to laugh. I shut the television off, drink some water, gag twice, and fall asleep. I wake up and it's morning. Another day passes. They take more blood, they bring more iced tea, I sit in the garden and try to fall asleep in the sun but can't. My wife lies in bed with me and curls in close and whispers in my ear, "We're halfway done. We're over halfway done," and the word *we're* echoes back in my head on and on and on and I wonder what her personal journey has been like—stress, anxiety, depression. I know and understand, logically and emotionally, that the three of us (myself, my wife, and my mother), are all on this train together and the train is spinning out of control for each of us in very different ways. While I feel hopeless, they feel helpless, unable to change anything or make a difference; they're forced to just sit down and watch.

Another night falls and another moon rises and there is a machine in the hall breathing for someone who I imagine is a man with stringy white

280

hair and translucent skin, his hands covered in liver spots, his eyes milky clouds. *Hufff . . . . Grrrr . . . . Hufffff . . . . Grrrrr . . . .*

I stare out the window into infinite space and pray, *"God, I am so scared. I could really use some courage here. Please let me know that you've got my back."*

I exhale and shut my eyes, and like a popular flood, sleep overtakes me.

Hospitals are like sitcoms; if you spend enough time with one you just start to see the same characters over and over again; nurses, doctors, janitors, lab techs, nutritionists. They are the cast and I . . . I *think* I'm the audience but maybe I'm just another character. Probably I'd be the super sexy dying kid in room 502 that all the really hot nurses are into and all the older nurses wish were their son. My character would be really modest, as well. Modest and sexy. And funny.

And strong.

Channing Tatum would probably have to play me in the televised movie version. Channing Tatum or maybe The Rock.

On today's episode there is a special-guest appearance by a new character. This is his only cameo, and I'll never see him again. The man knocks and enters, pushing a small cart. He's olive skinned, mid seventies, with tufts of white hair and deep lines set into his face like a cracked desert. I say, "Hello," and he smiles at me and I can tell by the lines in his face that he smiles often.

He sets the tray on my table and says, "How are you today, young man?" and I say, "I'm as good as I can be today," and he smiles and says, "That's absolutely wonderful," and then he turns around and leaves and I look at the clock and try to will it to move faster, hoping my mother and wife get here soon.

Hospitals are lonely places to be at with company. They're like a sarcophagus when you're alone.

I turn on the TV and immediately change my mind. I turn it off, turn my head, stare out the window. There's a racetrack somewhere over there, the Santa Anita Park. Jade and her mother had once walked over there at my request to "put $25 on the horse with the funniest name."

QuitYerBellyAchin cost me a pretty penny that day but I couldn't complain without thinking about the irony the name and situation bore me.

Through the open window I watch all manners of cars drive to work during morning rush hour: silver Chevy Cavaliers and white Dodge Dynasties and red convertibles and blue Bonnevilles, and I desperately wish that I were sitting in any of those automobiles and I desperately wish I were driving to a job on the other side of the city and I wish I were zoning out to NPR, my body on autopilot, trying to get through the week instead of trying to get through the moment. I wish I were excited about lunch instead of fearing it.

It is at this moment that a great and fantastic revelation washes over me and life is suddenly so very clear. I'm standing at such great heights and I'm looking down at the world and I can see everything from a different perspective and I can see that we are all very tiny and desperate.

In that moment I realize that I can do anything. And in that moment I swear that when I get better, I will make wiser decisions and I will have a job that I love and I will only be driven by passion. I think to myself, "I never want to forget this. Burn it into your brain, into your soul. It's easy to fall into routine. Keep it fresh. Stay sharp."

I feel alive and free.

And then I grab one of the six iced teas, lift it to my lips, and as the icy-cold liquid freezes my teeth, I feel something drop onto my lap that had been stuck to the bottom of the Styrofoam cup. Looking down I see a small rectangle that is the same size and shape as a business card. It's cream in color with a simple font on one side. There is no address guiding one to a further website or giving credit to any specific person or organization. It just says, "The Lord is Near to You."

I don't know what to make of that. I'm not saying it was a thing but I'm not *not* saying it was a thing. I'd spent collective weeks in the hospital previous to this moment and after this moment and I'd only ever seen this man this one time, directly on the coat tails of a prayer requesting a little pick-me-up juice from something bigger than me. What the "Bigger Than Me" thing is, I do not know. This is not meant to sway or convince anyone in relation to God or what that God may or may not. This is just me saying.

Several hours later my mother and wife arrive, both of them smelling like McDonald's pancakes. I show them the card and they each take turns holding it and staring at it and turning it over in their hands. My mother even smells it before pulling out *Yahtzee* and rolling dice and shout-whispering, "Full house! Two of a kind! Straight!" while I try to stare through the ceiling, through reality, through this world and this dimension; while I relax my eyes and try to see God. I let my mind slowly wander and everything is beautiful.

Dr. Yen, my oncologist, enters my room and I smile and greet her and she says, "Hi, Johnny. How you doing?" and she pushes her glasses up on her nose with that finger and she scrunches her face up and says, "How's mom and wife? Hospital food any good?" and I say, "They're good. This, not so much," and she says, "Yeah, I don't blame you. Everyone's on a budget and we gotta spend the good money on the medicine. It's not a Hilton, you know? *You know?*

It's just not—but the medicine—trust me—that's top of the line. It makes you feel sick, OK, you don't feel good, am I right? But it's getting the job done. If it's making you sick, imagine what it's doing to that cancer, OK?" and then she approaches me and pulls back the sheet and pulls up my gown and looks at my stitches where they removed my testicle and she says, "It's healing nicely, OK," and then she opens a manila envelope. I've learned that doctors and nurses only reference manila envelopes when they need to get the facts straight, when they're about to deliver a bomb and they need to make sure the proper grenade is going to the proper person.

She scans her finger down something—a chart, numbers, information—and I shut my eyes and focus on the texture of the card in my hand and then she says words that I will never forget.

She says, "OK, it looks here like your cancer is gone," and my mother drops the dice onto the floor and her hands go to her lips and someone squeezes my hand and I look down and see my wife and everything is moving in slow motion and the clock is making thundering TICK-TOCKS and my lips curl back and it's the first time I've cried because I've been happy in a very long time because it's the first time I've actually been happy in a very long time.

I choke out, "Thank you, thank you," and she says, "Yes, uh, that's it. It's all gone but we're going to, uh, we're going to do one more round of chemo just to be safe, just to make sure. It's 100% gone but we, uh, in this case we *do* want to beat a dead horse. The cancer is the dead horse, not you, even though you, uh, probably feel like one. Am I right? Am I right? You're very much alive and will hopefully stay that way for a very long time," and I lift my hand to my face and I wipe away tears and I nod and I say, "Yes. Thank you . . . " and I squeeze the card in my hand until my knuckles turn white.

Dr. Yen leaves and the three of us just stare at one another, knowing that words can only spoil it.

PART 4

"The sun is gone, but I have a light."
–Kurt Cobain

CHAPTER 34
ICE CREAM

I'm lying in my living room, completely healed, cancer free, and asking myself, "Is this remission?" because I still feel naked and exposed and vulnerable. I still feel sick and there's still a bucket resting on the floor next to me.

I've been home for one day, and even with the good news, great news, fantastic news, it's the worst day yet. I'm still bearing the weight of five months of chemotherapy and my mind and body are just as atrophied as ever and the world around me is still *too much* and *too intense* to comprehend. Everything is still flooding. I am still drowning in poison. The battle is no longer me versus cancer. It's now me versus chemo. I'm a contestant on the world's worst episode of *Fear Factor*. Joe Rogan says, *"Can he take one more round of chemotherapy!?"* and my competitors are all trying to slam me and say things like, "He looks like that skeleton in biology classrooms!" and, "He ain't got game!" and, "Bitch needs to go hooooome," and I wish so badly that I could just walk off this really terrible game show and simply give up.

Outside of my house, crawling down the street at a slug's pace, I can hear the ice-cream man and his filthy truck slithering toward all the kiddies. His speaker and stereo have been broken the entire time we've lived in this house so his music always sounds like a predatory warning more than a cheerful welcome. He's the ice-cream man in a Wes Craven film. I hear his music and always picture him smoking rolled cigarettes, yellow teeth, yellow eyes, totally emaciated, some junkie pushing dairy.

The "music" gets louder and louder, the speaker scratching and popping, hissing and whining, the tune slowing down and speeding up, the music bending like a warped record. It's elevator music leading to Dante's inferno.

I shut my eyes and tell myself that he'll be gone in a moment. I tell myself to just hang on, to just breathe, to just pray, to just focus on something, anything. I put a pillow over my head but I can still hear the noise, the sound, boring into my brain, into the center of me, into my veins, my soul. It's pushing me against the wall and cracking me open and breaking me and I can't get away from it and it's not going to make me puke but it is going to destroy me if he stops and then he does stop. He stops right outside my house, right outside my window, and the tune plays over and over and over and over and over again, looping on loops on loops, breaking and bending, warping and warbling, slowing and speeding. No children are approaching the van. The siren wails and screams, and then it does break me and I wish I could explain this to you better than I am but I also hope you never understand. I wish I could reach into your brain and into your stomach and squeeze your nuts until you cough up blood and twist the knife so you know what it feels like, how the music makes me feel, how the chemo makes me feel, how the poison makes me feel, how the medicine makes me feel, because it's not an ice-cream truck, it's an Ice-Cream Truck and it's like one of those horrible ones from *Maximum Overdrive* or one of the Decepticons and I know it has ultimate intelligence and it knows that I'm in here and its sole purpose and intention is to do only one thing and that one thing is to seek and destroy.

Me.

And then the missile, the A-Bomb, the C-chord, the broken and beaten tune sniffs me out and finds me and I am done. I break down and I weep uncontrollably, and it's not because I'm sad and it's not because I'm sick and it's not because I'm depressed but it's because of the Ice-Cream Truck and that music and it hurts so bad in such a foreign way and I am drowning.

Someone touches my shoulder and I pull the blanket down and pull the pillow off my head and pull my hood back and take off my hat and open my eyes and Jade is standing there and she says, "Are you—oh . . . . Are you crying?" and I say, "The . . . ice-cream truck! It's trying to kill me!" and she says, "Are you high?" and I say, "No," and she says, "Do you want to be?" and I roll off the couch and caterpillar myself into the kitchen. Jade carries my cocoon behind me and wraps me back up in My Yellow Chair.

My wife sets the machine down in front of me and I begin to examine the plastic tube while my mother grinds the plant like an apothecary. Where it was once translucent and clean, it's now become discolored with muck the shade of infected urine. Whether that's from the plant or the burn, I'm not certain, but I have to stop and wonder if my throat looks like an organic replica.

I mindlessly rub my Adam's apple and intentionally cough up something deep down. Unwilling to swallow it I spit it into my puke bucket. Brown.

Something grotesque wafts under my nose and I turn my face away. Some repugnant scent; something bitter and acrid; something . . . I lift my arm . . . it's me. I turn my head and look in the mirror and I am truly one mottled beard away from looking like a wilderness person.

My wife says, "John?" and I say, "Huh? Yes?" and she says, "What's wrong?" and I say, "I . . . need a bath," and she says, "A *bath*?" and I say, "Yeah . . . I smell like shit," and she stands up and walks out of the room and I hear the bathtub turn on and I hear the octaves of aqua slowly rise and she comes back and holds out her hand and I stand up and she supports me into the bathroom where steam rises out of the small pool.

She shuts the door behind me and she unzips my coat and pulls it off my shoulders and lets it fall to the ground, revealing my true size. She pulls my hat off, revealing my smooth skull. She pulls my shirt off, revealing my ribs and emaciated arms. She unbuckles my belt and pulls off my pants, revealing my hairless legs and finally, she pulls off my underwear, revealing my scar. I take one step onto the scale and she says, "Don't . . . " and I say, "Wait . . . " and I see that I am 130 pounds completely stark naked. I am the same weight as a large dog, a Great Dane. I am the same weight as a high-school girl.

I look at myself in the mirror and I suddenly see me. Not the way I have seen myself, which is in such minute changes that I haven't *seen* change but I suddenly see myself as I was and now as I am, two people at once. I see a stranger. I see a disease. I see struggle and I see . . . Survival.

I see Bruce Willis at the end of *Die Hard* covered in blood and bruises, broken glass stuck in his feet. I see Bruce Campbell at the end of *Army of Darkness*, covered in filth and pelted by evil. I see Bruce Springsteen.

I am The Boss.

I turn and step off the scale and Jade holds my geriatric elbow as I step into the steaming water and lower my smelly body into the scented fragrance and perfumes and soaps and steams and I say, "Thank you," and she says, "You're welcome," and then she picks up a washcloth and dips it in the water and begins to scrub my back and my chest and my legs

293

and here I am, I realize, at my weakest and my most vulnerable. So far, anyway.

She points to my bicep, or, at the very least, the place on my arm where my bicep should be and says, "What is this?" I look down and see dark brown striations running underneath my skin that look like tiger scratches or stretch marks. I exhale and say, "Oh, yeah, I forgot to mention those. The chemo is burning my skin from the inside."

So small is this on the full scale of weirdness that it doesn't even warrant further conversation from either of us.

She runs the washcloth over the marks (which don't wash off), over my head and over my face and the water runs down my chin and I think that five months ago I was a pothead driving to Las Vegas, screaming on the freeway and singing at the top of my lungs, watching the sun rise, the biggest concern in my life a job that I didn't enjoy.

Five months.

Like a car accident, it all happened so fast and spun out of control so quickly; it all came out of nowhere and suddenly I was thrust over the steering wheel and I was crashing through the windshield and falling and falling and falling until my wife is giving me a sponge bath because I can't do it myself. An ice-cream truck reduces me to tears. I don't recognize myself.

Five months.

Water trickles off my chin and I try to look into the future. I try to gaze five months down the road. Chemotherapy will be done, remission will have begun, my mom will have gone home, I will have gone back to work and . . . it all seems like an intangible impossibility. None of it seems likely or possible or even probable.

I say, "Do you think this will end?" and Jade says, "Soon," and I say, "It seems weird, doesn't it? Going back to normal," and Jade says, "Things will never be normal again," and I nod and grunt and she scrubs my knees and my feet and I say, "We'll never be the same, will we?" and she says, "No," and then, "I hope not," and I grunt again, glad that she is having her own revelations.

She says, "I want to travel more," and I say, "I want to camp more," and she says, "I want a family," and I say, "Me too," and then everything is silent except for the dripping water until I say, "One drip at a time," and she says, "Yeah . . . we did it . . . one drip at a time. Only a few bags left," and I shudder to think that it's over but we're not done. My tears mix with the water running down my face and the thought of another round is so unbearable that I have to push it from my mind and focus on the victory at hand.

She pushes her forehead against my ear and whispers, "I love you," and I say, "Thank you," and she says, "For what?" and I say, "Everything. For staying. For helping. For just . . . the doctors, the files, the organizing, the appointments, the medicines, the charts, the insurance, the fights with the hospital, with the nurses, with the doctors, with *me*. Thank you for just . . . everything. I don't know what I would have done if you weren't here. I really don't. I'm so thankful for you and I hope I never have to be on your end. I hope you never have to be on my end. I hope this is it and you've just been . . . incredible. I love you," and when I look over she has tears running down her face and so I say, "Hey! We're both crying!" and she says, "You're—" *sob,* "not crying . . . " and I say, "No!" *Sob!* "I am! I was just hiding my tears in the water! It was total espionage because I didn't—" *sob*, "want you to know it!" and then she says, "You're an idiot," and I say, "I—" *sob,* "know," and then she hands me a towel and I walk out of the bathroom smelling less like sulfur and more like a Starbucks winter-themed drink—pumpkin latte or cinnamon mochaccino.

CHAPTER 35
MY BLOODY VALENTINE

Days pass like kidney stones. *Dr. Oz* is playing and so I think it must be around noon. I want to push the TV off the shelf. I hate how standardized it is. I hate how scheduled it is. I hate how predictable the entire process is. I hate that everyone on the TV is so happy and falsely charming and plastic. I hate them gazing out at me, into my house, not seeing me but trying to talk to me, give me advice, counsel me, imagining that they, the daytime teevees, know everything that the world is going through; the details, the minutia, the process.

My hormones are going off the wall and through the roof. My testicle (both my testicles) are missing and I'm angry and then I'm sad. I tell my mom that I love her and then I want to break a vase but only one that's owned by a person that pronounces it *vozz*. I cover my head with a blanket and just want to be left alone in the silence. I want to paint my nails black, embrace death, and write gothic poetry about moonbeams, dark angels, and religious sacrifices. I shut my eyes and try to logically explain to myself that *I'm not upset or happy or sad*, it's all *hormones*. It's all just a *chemical reaction in my brain and your brain is misfiring left and right*. I would see a piece of vanilla cake and want to cut it with a knife . . . but not to eat it. I just want to hurt it because it's pretty.

I begin to feel as though my emotions (like everything else) are outside of my control. Imagine you're at your workplace and you're doing a phenomenal job and you *have been* doing a phenomenal job for a year or two. You're at the absolute top of your game, proud of your achievements and when raise time comes around, you go into your boss's office and he fires you on the spot for not performing at company standards.

So, of course, you're really mad. You're furious at him and at the company. *And that's fine because those feelings are totally normal for that circumstance.*

Now imagine you're sitting on a beach and you've got the place totally to yourself, with nice weather, good food, a special someone. You sit back, pull out a beer, and then you feel that horrible flood of emotions mentioned above. They're not tied to anything; there is no event, past or present. They just show up randomly and you want to hiss and fight.

When you lose control of your hormones, you lose control of yourself. You become a slave to their chemical whims and it's very scary because it all happens at a moment's notice.

So I stand up and coast slowly into the bathroom where I remove my shirt, pull out my AndroGel-steroid-hormone-medication pump (or, My New Testicles) and apply two full squirts of the gel onto my shoulder blades. It quickly dissipates into a sticky residue that I have to let dry on my skin, covering me in a thin sheen that "no one is allowed to touch under any circumstances. Doctor's orders."

I hobble back into the dining room just as *Dr. Oz* is ending and I stare at him with his chiseled features and his piercing eyes and his charming smile and voice like buttered bread and I say, "If I ever meet you, I'm going to bite your ear off," and then it's 12:30 and he's gone and something else comes on and the television is just as predictable as—something unexpectedly moves past the living room window in a dark blur. It's outside and it was quick but I saw it, whatever *it* was. I say, "Uh . . . Jade," and she says, "Yeah?" and I look over at my mom and she says, very sheepishly, "What? What? Whaaaaaat?" and I say, "Who is here?" and Jade says, "Someone is here? I need to pick up the house!" and then I hear footsteps whose tone, weight, and cadence immediately harkens me back to my childhood. There's a sudden knock on the door. It's brief but with a level of force that I recognize.

When I see that both Jade and my mother are waiting for me to get up and answer the door, I simply do so vocally. "Come in!" The doorknob twists and in walk my sister and dad.

I stand up in a state of shock, my nipples hard from the cold air, my frame an old flannel on a wire hanger. My sister and dad approach me, both smiling, knowing they've surprised me. My sister reaches me first and throws out her arms but I jerk backward and

299

throw up my hands as though I were fending off a mugger, screaming something that sounds like, "*I-wahh-kooo!*" which is not so much a word as it is a guttural noise that translates roughly to, "Don't touch me, I'm wearing AndroGel Man Poison."

I tell my sister that if she were to touch me she'd grow a mustache and so I instead stick out my arm, shaking hands with her. She stares at me and grips my hand and tears suddenly fill her eyes and I say, "Thanks for coming," and she, never good with words but always full of emotions, croaks out, "Yes, yes, of course. Always. Anything. Wouldn't miss it." I release her hand and step around her to my father, who I've never seen eye to eye with. I stick out my hand and he embraces me and I say, "Thank you for coming," and he says, "How do you feel?" and I say, "Good . . . . That's a lie. I'm sick." He releases me and I wander back to My Yellow Chair, slip down into it, cover myself up with a blanket and shut my eyes while my dad speaks, always in his precise and succinct military fashion.

"We drove all day yesterday and then all night. Stopped in a Kmart parking lot and slept for two and a half hours and then kept going. Made it from South Dakota to California in record time; twenty-one and a half hours!"

This is my dad. These are his passions. Personal time trials.

He asks what we want to do today and I shut my eyes and say, "This is it," and he says, "You guys wanna go to the beach?" and I say, "No," and he says, "Car museum?" and I say, "I can't walk." He purses his lips and I say, "Welcome to the suck."

My dad sits down next to me, unfolds a newspaper, and begins to read. My sister sits at the table and texts her boyfriend. And so goes the rest of the day.

*** *** *** *** ***

Cancer made me into an agoraphobic. I was afraid to go anywhere, everywhere, because, and I know I've probably mentioned this to death, my sudden trigger vomiting was so powerful and out of control that I was afraid I would be caught in public without access to a restroom. My home was my comfort zone and I didn't want to leave it for fear of being caught in the open.

My home was my sanctuary.

The following day we go out for Mexican food and then to an early show of *My Bloody Valentine* in 3-D. For ninety minutes, I sit between my dad and sister and watch naked chicks get hacked to pieces. The movie was my choice and I regretted every minute of it. As the credits begin to roll I feel my stomach turn over and I stand up and say, "I think . . . I'm going to be sick," and my mom says, "OK, we're leaving," and I say, "No . . . I'm going to be sick right now," and people are sort of just shuffling in the aisles like lost sheep stupidly grazing and I'm about to heave and puke and when it happens I know, I can just feel it, that it's not going to stop, it's going to roll and wave and heave and push and pour and nothing within a 15-foot radius will be safe from my spray and so I shout the word, "MOVE!" and everyone does. Everyone in the entire row sits down or steps aside and I run with the undiscovered fusion energy of an atom bomb. I leap over laps, hurdle seats, lunge down stairs, race up the inclined aisle, marathon down the halls, find the restrooms, kick open the doors, push pass a group of people in line, shove past a man just entering the stall and just as I say, "Excuse m—" it all comes up, red and yellow and brown and lumpy like potatoes, again and again and again, spittle and saliva and bile hanging from my lips and pouring from my nose. My hands clutch the handicap rails and I hate everything about this. I'm angry at myself for puking, for vomiting, for not being able to keep it together.

There's a very internal struggle happening wherein I start to get very angry at myself and pick and peck and poke and say, "You pussy. You pussy. Get your shit together. Pull it together," and I puke again and it's cherry red and I don't know what I've eaten but it just looks like more blood. I wish more than anything that I were just at home, back in the comforts of my four walls, my territory, my familiar space; back in My Yellow Chair, under my jacket; back on the couch, under a blanket; in my bed.

Somewhere where "making a scene" is not considered "making a scene."

You know you're amongst close family when you can puke in front of them and they all just keep eating dinner like nothing happened.

I heave again and a tear runs down my face, dropping into the toilet. My stomach feels like it's tearing open and I push my knuckles against the cold tile wall. My legs shake and I bend down, proposing to Queen Porcelain, my knees instantly soaking with the piss of strangers.

I hate what I've become.

I hear a door open and I dry heave and cough and dry heave and cover my hand over my mouth and wipe my lips on my sleeve and push my face into my shoulder and I just want to weep. I hate being such a convalescent. *I am twenty-six years old. I should be in peak health!*

There's a tap on the bathroom stall and my dad says, "Are you OK?" and I say, "No . . . but . . . yeah. I'll be out in just a minute," and he says, "OK," and then I hear him take a few steps away from the door and wait.

My father and I have never been emotionally close and so I anticipate him waiting for me in the hallway, taking the extra ten steps and giving me that "casual privacy" you would offer to someone who is sick. But instead he sits on the sink and waits and suddenly the bathroom isn't so bad.

CHAPTER 36
TONGUE

When I open my eyes, moonlight is still shining through my windows and my wife's breathing is still soft and rhythmic. I know I won't get back to sleep so I just Imagine. When there is nothing to do, it's all there is. When everything is gone outside, when your body has been reduced to rubble, when your emotions are running rampant and every thought clouds your brain with fog, all you can do is Imagine.

I focus in on one single thing, one detail, one moment, one idea and I circle around it, staring at it, examining it and dissecting it. The thought this morning is My Fourth Round. I try to Imagine what one level deeper will look like; I Imagine it as a deep sub-basement. A cellar. There aren't many people here and those who shuffle around in the darkness are pale and sinewy. I Imagine a nurse in the not-too-distant future pulling an IV out of my arm and saying, "All right, you're done," and then I Imagine walking out of the hospital and entering into the sunlight and feeling alive and free and while I lie there in the darkness, in my True Reality, everything still seems far away and unattainable.

People say to me, "One more round! Just one more round! The light is at the end of the tunnel!" and I see the light but it doesn't look like it's getting any closer. I understand that time is passing but why does it have to happen in *Matrix* bullet time?

I push my blankets back and drape my legs over the edge of the bed. I need to pee. I stand up and take a deep breath and my wife turns over and says, "Are you OK?" She's like a mother with a new baby, sensing every movement in the silence. I say, "Yeah. Just gotta pee, " and I smile and she says, "Shout if you need something," and I smile again, open the bedroom door and exit.

Walking through the darkened house, I hear a faint *click-click-click* of computer keys and round a corner where I find my dad sitting at our dining-room table doing work remotely on his laptop, a twice filled bowl of Cocoa Puffs next to him. He looks up and smiles but doesn't say anything. I say, "Hi," and, "What time is it?" and he says, "Seven a.m. my time. I've been up for two hours," and I nod, and doing the simple math, figure it must be around 5 a.m. here. I pee and walk into the kitchen and he keeps typing without looking up.

I want to sit down at the table and speak to him and ask him what he's doing or ask him *how* he's doing or ask something, anything that will fill the silence in the kitchen. *Click-click-click.*

I open up the cabinets and the fridge, searching for food that I won't eat; some repressed muscle memory pushing me on, not wanting to face the fact that I don't fully know the man sitting in my dining room even though I've lived in the same house with him my entire life. I open up a cupboard filled with frying pans and just stare at them, trying to look busy. I say, "What are you working on?" and he says, "Building my website," and I say, "Ah." I pull out a box of Cinnamon Toast Crunch and a bowl before putting them both away. I consider going back to the bedroom but the darkness in there is just too heavy and I know I'll drown in it. I end up sitting down at the table and staring at the back of his laptop, at the glowing logo. I say, "What's your website about?" and he says, "Cars I'm working on . . . building stuff." *Click-click-click*.

I am dealing with complete anarchy in my personal life and pushing forward every single day, one step further, one step further, one step further and here I am, sitting at a table in an empty house with my biological father and I have no idea how to confront this situation. I have no idea what to say, what to do. I try to make a joke but neither of us laughs. I start to feel funny (*strange*, not *haha*) and just lie my head in my hands. He asks if I'm OK and I say, "Sometimes."

My sister enters the room. My mother enters the room. My wife enters the room. Cereal is made. Oatmeal is made. Toast is made. Orange juice is poured. My sister sits down next to me and says, "What are you doing?" and I say, "What am I doing-what? What do you mean?" and she says, "Your tongue is kind of a weird color," and when I examine myself in the mirror I see that it is indeed the same shade as raw beef that's been left in the sun for too long. My wife says, "Do we need to go to the hospital?" and I turn on her like a corner and say,

307

"No, no, no. No hospitals. No emergency rooms. No nothing," and my dad says, "If we need to take you to the hospital, you will go. I will overpower you. I can overpower you," and I understand now, today, what he meant, but at the time it inflamed my emotions. Even though it sounds like a joke, he wasn't messing around. He wasn't being coy. He genuinely meant what he said. He would bear hug me and drag me kicking and screaming to the E.R. if it's what my wife said I needed.

I turn on him next and say, with as much acidity as I can muster, "You touch me and I will fight you." At first glance this looks like the eternal power struggle between father and son, a story as old as time, but on second glance it's just my struggle. To control something. Anything. He raises an eyebrow and looks at Jade, who looks at me and so I say, "The E.R. is a waste of time. We're going to show up, sit in a waiting room for two hours. They're going to draw some blood and tell me to hydrate. I don't need a replay of *The Adventures of Blood Vomit*. I don't *need* Christmas Eve take two. I don't *need* to stay another night there. What I *need* is to relax and take it easy. I did it your way last time and it was a total bust and now we're doing it my way. This time *it's my turn*."

Grasping at control.

Jade never answers. Instead she just exhales deeply and turns away. My dad turns back to his laptop. My sister's phone buzzes and she reads a text. I say, "Who's that?" and she says, "None of yer bizzznus," and I say, "Is it your boyfriend? Is it that

308

guy I met? Is it Jes?" and she glances at my dad—
click-click-click—and makes wide eyes at me that
seem to say, *Shut up!* So I do. She texts something
back and I say, "What did you just text him back?
Was that Jes you were texting? That guy you were
dating? The guy I met?" and she says, "I told you to
shut up," and then she walks outside.

I met Jes about a year previous and we'd only
spoken on two separate occasions. He was a nice
enough fellow but had recently, I guess, gotten
involved in and charged with conspiracy to
manufacture marijuana and was going to be doing
some prison time. No one was really sure which
members of our family knew or did not know so my
sister was very sensitive about the subject being
broached at all. My extended family is full of strange
secrets and double-crosses and so most things,
regardless of how lacking in logic, are just taken with
a grain of salt.

I stand up and move to My Yellow Chair
before closing my eyes. I've been up for about two
hours and it's starting to make me feel strange, light
headed. I say, "Church this morning?" and my mother
says, "Yes," and my wife says, "If you're OK," and
my sister is outside, and my dad goes *click-click-
click*.

I shut my eyes and nap.

When I wake up there is an electric movement
in the air that says *something is happening. Grab your*

things, c'mon, let's go! It's time! I slide my feet into a pair of old yellow sneakers and stand up. "I'm ready."

My mother spruces her hair up. My wife spritzes herself with perfume. My sister changes shirts and jeans and shoes and then shirts again and then ties her hair back and then lets it down. I feel strange again but, since feeling strange has become a complete recurring theme in my life, I simply ignore it and soldier on.

We all gather by the front door and my mother says, "Mike, are you ready to go?" and my dad looks up from his computer and says, "Huh?" and my mother says, "To church? We're leaving," and he goes c*lick-click-click . . . CLICK*, and then shuts his laptop and we all walk out the door.

In the car I lay my head against the glass and feel the bumps in the road gyrate my skull and shake my brain. Next to me I can hear my sister *click-click-clicking* on her BlackBerry, every button a stapler to the temple. The problem with those phones is that even if you silence the "clicking sound" feature, those buttons are just built to click. *Click-click-click! CLICK-CLICK-CLICK! CLLIIICCCKK!! Click-click-click.*

I turn to my sister and say, "How is work?" and she starts to tell me about her job and about how she thinks her boss doesn't like her and how she's thinking about quitting and all the scandalous things that happen there and I nod politely and ask questions

310

and in the front seat my dad says, "These billboards are all in Spanish. I can't read Spanish. Wait, I think that one says something about the number three… and maybe something about a burrito." I say, "That's El Pollo Loco."

My sister says, "So what are you going to do when you go back? Back to work? Are you going to have the same job or what?" and truly, truly, it's a fear that has weighed on my heart since this first happened, since this all began. *What next?*

Will I be able to just jump back into my career, back into my job? Will I be able to sit in an edit bay for ten hours a day after knowing that death is imminent? Will I be able to commute an hour each way and wile away in a cube while my life escapes through me one moment at a time? I don't know.

I don't think so.

When I am released back into the world I want to break the social norms and destroy the constraints and I want to live by a set of guidelines that work for me because, quite frankly, the ones I've been using aren't really blowing my hair back. I don't think humans were meant to live like caged chickens and . . . .

. . . I begin to speak; to relay these thoughts to Theresa. I begin to pour my heart out, wearing my fear on my sleeve like a patch. I turn my head and glance back out the window but continue to talk. The words are coming easier and easier, the fears becoming easier to speak about. It feels good to get it off my chest and then, suddenly, my sister just blurts out, in the loudest voice I've ever heard, the word, "HOLA!"

That's what she says. She says, "HOLA!" and she nearly shouts it, like she's welcoming the Chilean soccer team back to their home country after winning a major victory. "HOLA!"

I turn my head to put this interruption into context and I see her . . . on her phone. It was on silent so I didn't hear it ring. Apparently I had just been talking to myself. I look into the front seat and see my mom and dad both staring straight ahead in silence.

I am pouring out my heart to the world passing by. I say, "Are you *kidding me*?!" and my sister says, "What?" and I say, "I'm sitting here talking to you and—" she just holds a finger up over her lips and says, "Shhh."

How dare you shush me! My brain explodes in rage and indignation and I raise my fist in the air, but my sister merely mocks me. I whisper-shout, "You think the cancer kid can't beat you up?! You think I can't take you down?! Well, you're probably right but I'm going to remember this! *All* of this! HOLA, in*deed!*" and then she puts her finger to her mouth and shushes me again, violently, truly wanting me to hush.

312

I say, "*Who are you talking to*?" and she mouths, "Shut up! Jes," and I say, "Jes? Jes, your boyfriend? Jes, the guy you're dating? Jes, the guy I met?" I pause and then say, "Give me the phone . . . . "

Theresa glares at me, unsure how to accept this challenge. She knows we'd met before (twice) and she knows that we got along all right (twice) but she has no idea why it is I would want to talk to this man after having not seen him for close to a year.

She says, into the phone, "My brother . . . wants to talk to you . . . . I don't know . . . . I don't know . . . . Is that OK? OK." And then she holds out the phone and I reach out for it but she pulls it away at the last minute, leaving me grasping at air. I say, "What?" and she just raises her fist in the air, mocking me again and says, "I'm serious."

I push the mobile device to my ear and say, "Hello. Jes?" And he mumbles something, sounding unsure, unsure of our conversation, unsure of himself, unsure of everything. I say, "What's going on?" and he says, "You know, not much, uh . . . . "

We sit in silence for a moment and then I say, "So, you're going away for a bit?" and he agrees and my sister slaps the palm of her hand against her face. I turn my head and look out the window and I say, "I just wanted to say that I think we're both going through something very unusual and I hope that when we come out the other end we can be very different

313

people. I hope these things change us for the better and uh . . . keep it together, man," and he says, "Oh . . . uh . . . thanks. Thank you," and I say, "See ya," and hand the phone back to my sister who just stares at me for a moment before speaking into it and saying, "Hello . . . hi. Yeah . . . I don't . . . know . . . . "

Years later, the two of them will be married and I'll stand up for them at their wedding, not simply because they asked me to but because I believe in their marriage. Prison will affect and change Jes in fantastic ways and when he comes out of the darkness, he will be a new man, ready to embrace life for himself. Today he's one of the kindest, most thoughtful people I know and I would put my personal reputation on the line for him at any turn.

Life has a very funny way of changing us.

We take the Highland exit and I mentally take note of the spot where I slipped into my grand mal seizure. I don't know it then, but I'll red flag it for the rest of my life. A mile up and I take another mental note of the spot where I woke up. I mark the trees, the light poles, the bus stop. I sigh and everything swims in front of me for a moment but then is gone. A few miles later we hang a right on Wilshire and pull into the parking lot of the church.

My family shuffles down the sidewalk, I leading the way for a change. I turn around, perhaps too quickly, and say, "Remember to silence your cell phones," and everyone reaches into their pockets to do so. When I turn back around I feel something in the very furthest recess of my brain, a white mist. Then I feel something in my toes.

We enter the lobby and find ourselves standing in a throng of individuals. I've just walked a block and am feeling extremely exhausted . . . far more tired than I have any right to be, even in my present state. I think, "Something is not right. I need . . . to sit . . . down."

I take two steps toward a support column in the center of the room and that white mist suddenly makes a lunging maneuver from the back of my brain and circles around to the front. The feeling in my toes shoots up my legs and into my thighs and everything is becoming a strange water-color painting.

My wife says, "Are you all—"

And then I feel my knees buckle and the weight of the world is on my shoulders—every screaming child, every warring nation, every lusting adult. Every prayer is being shoveled on top of me and I'm slowly drowning. God reaches down, grabs the room and spins it like a top (or perhaps a dreidel, depending on your religious orientation) and my right foot shoots out to establish my balance and my left foot shoots forward to counter.

Someone says something else and I'm trying to stand up but it's all so heavy and spinning and then the words are just electrical motor engines and the darkness on my brain consumes my eyeballs and the world around me fades . . . to . . . black.

*** *** *** *** ***

When I open my eyes it takes a few moments for my reality to click on but when it does, it's just like a light; everything is illuminated. I'm here, the church, the people, the embarrassment. *Don't be embarrassed*! But I am, I'm lying on a floor in a room filled with strangers who are all staring at me. *Drink this*! A cup of water. Great. I would love to throw this up in front of you all when I'm nice and ready. *Don't stand up*! Great, I'll just hang out down here. *Just lay down*! No. Absolutely not. I will *not* look as though I'm taking a nap in the center of the floor. I understand what happened here was a little weird and everyone is a little freaked out but I don't need to lie down. I am a grown-ass man.

I sit up Indian style and say, "Jade, please help me up," and my dad says, "Just hang on, John," and I say, "Help me . . . *up*," and they do because, unless they're going to pin me down, I'm not lying here like Lieutenant Dan.

My sister says, "Whoa. Your tongue is . . . really *white*," and I say, "What do you mean, *white*?" and the rest of the my family suddenly makes a noise like a vampire seeing a cross and even a couple of people standing next to me take a small step back. My wife snaps a photo on her phone and shows it to me.

Oh, I think, *they meant* white. *Like paper. Or snow. Or a ghost.* My tongue had been drained of all color and now it just looked like someone had shoved one of those weird albino dog turds between my lips.

I clap my hands together and say, "Well . . . so . . . to the hospital then?" and without any verbal agreement, we all just turn and start walking back to the car.

CHAPTER 37
AND
IF I
DON'T
SIGN?

I can't believe that the emergency room has a waiting room. I mean, I get it but . . . you just would not believe the lines in the Los Angeles E.R. It rivals the DMV. It truly does.

After two predictable hours of mentally dissecting Georgia O'Keeffe paintings (*How did she get a corner on the medical market*??) we're finally called into a private room where they deduce that I need another blood transfusion, "*But*," the nurse tells me far too casually, "Before we can get to that, we're going to need you to sign these contracts here, here, here, and here, Mr. Brookbank." I grab the pen and say, "Oh . . . kay . . . . What is this for? What am I signing?" and the nurse says, "Just in case you get AIDS from this blood you can't sue us," and I say, "EXCUSE ME?" The nurse laughs and says, "The chances are very small—I mean, less than one percent," and I say, "Nothing to do with you but, honestly, my luck has been pretty shady lately so, just to abate my own curiosity, would you mind walking me through your screening process before potentially pumping me chock full of AIDS blood?"

The nurse says, "Someone comes in and gives blood—small vial. We test that blood. If it's clear, we ask them to come back—typically a day or two later—and this is when we'll take several bags of it."

I say, "OK, go on."

And the nurse says, "Well, it's possible that they contracted AIDS in those two days."

And I say, "That's not the end of your screening process? You test the blood again, yes?"

And she says, "Yes, we do but . . . there is always room for human error and that's where *this*—" and her finger pokes the contract, "comes in."

I say, "I see," and look at my wife who says, "If he gets AIDS—I mean, if you give him AIDS—what does that mean?"

And the nurse says, "Well, he will have AIDS."

And my wife says, "Yes, I'm clear on that but . . . we have no follow through? He just has AIDS? You're not held responsible?"

And the nurse says, "Not if you sign that contract."

And so I say, "And what if I don't sign the contract?"

And the nurse says, "Then you can't have any of our blood."

And I say, "Any of your AIDS blood?"

And she says, "Any of our blood at all, AIDS or otherwise."

And I say, "Cold move."

And the nurse says, "I know. I just work here."

So I sign the paperwork and the nurse says, "Good choice. I'll be back to get you in a bit," and then she leaves us.

In the waiting area where we're all staged sits a large black woman with a cast on her foot. I see her all by herself looking nervous and so I direct my chauffer to the given target and Theresa begins to slowly wheel me over to her. I say, "You waiting to get your blood drawn?" and she nods and I say, "What happened to your foot?" and she says she slipped and fell and broke it. I grimace and say, "Could be worse," and she says, "Oh, not being able to walk is pretty bad enough," and I laugh and say, "But it could be worse so you're pretty lucky," and then I say, "Hey, I'm afraid of needles. How about you go in there before me and when you come out, you tell me if the nurse is any good. If she's shoddy I'll request someone new." The woman nods and agrees and laughs.

She says, "Are you getting your blood drawn, too?" and I say, "Yeah," and she says, "I hate them needles," and I say, "I know. That's why you need to be the guinea pig. I don't want to get jabbed a bunch. You gotta take one for the team," and she laughs and says, "Why you here?" which is a pretty invasive question and so I cough a couple times, really hard, into my fist and say, "I've got this really contagious disease that they're still trying to figure out. It's like the bird flu but with no remedy. It's airborne." I sniff really loudly and then cough into my sleeve and say, "Sorry." The woman slowly pushes her wheelchair back and says, "Maybe you . . . should have one of those masks or . . . " and I say, "Yeah, I basically live in a bubble at my house – like a little plastic tent. But once in a while I get to come out. I'm just not supposed to be very close to people. You should be fine," and then I cough into my hand again and simply look at the floor, in silence.

Behind me, I can feel my sister touch my shoulder. She's not very good at this sort of game so I'm sure she's very uncomfortable right now. I look up at the woman and smile and she smiles back with a mouth full of fear and weirdly friendly eyes that seem to say, "Act natural. Act *naturaaaaal* . . . . " And then I start to laugh and I say, "I'm just kidding!" and she laughs as well and my sister releases a burst of awkward laughter and then I say, "I was actually at church—that's my family over there. We were over at church this morning and I was standing in the lobby and suddenly everything just went dark. I passed out. When I woke up, my tongue was white." I stick it out and she pulls her lips back in open disgust and says, "Ick." I say, "Thank you, yes, I know," and she starts to laugh again and says, "You passed out in *church*?" and I say, "Yeah, right there," and she says, "Boy, I bet they all thought you were having a *gen-u-wine religious experience!*" and then she has a mock seizure. She says, "Why do you think that happened?" and I say, "Well . . . I have cancer," and she says, "*Oh, OK. Yes. CANCER*. I get it. You're like Mr. Funny Guy, huh? Do they keep you in a cancer bubble at home?" and my sister and I both stare at her dead pan and I say, "There is no such thing as a cancer bubble."

A long moment passes before the woman says, "Oh, dear," and then I laugh and say, "It's OK. I actually don't have cancer anymore but I'm still in chemotherapy," and then a nurse enters and calls the black woman's name. The two of them disappear into a back room and reappear moments later, tape now stitched around the woman's arm joint. I say, "How is she?" and she says, "It was fast," and I say, "Good."

The black woman looks at me and says, "God bless you," and I say, "Didn't you hear me? I said I don't have cancer anymore."

*** *** *** *** ***

Two floors up I'm getting another blood transfusion; the platelets are draining back into my body like a soggy hourglass. My wife clicks through the TV. Nothing is on and we watch all of it.

This is the first time that cancer has proven to me that, just because it's gone, it's not vanquished. Just because it's out of sight, doesn't mean it's out of mind. Cancer is the king who, once dead, you realize has booby-trapped the whole palace.

I stick out my tongue and say, "What color is it?" My sister looks up from her phone and says, "Pink," and I know I've won another battle and I'm also certain that the war is coming to an end. I just have to wonder how much PTSD is going to come along with it.

A few days later everything is back to "normal." My dad is clicking away on his laptop, my sister is nowhere to be found, my wife is at work for the day, and my mother is making random notes on napkins, a habit she's exhibited my entire life. On every vacation she takes she'll find herself a pen along with a napkin or some form of old scrap paper and begin jotting down short-hand journal entries. I can only assume it's some form of coping mechanism.

As I walk past her I look down at the paper and read: *dad & t arrive / movie / popcorn w caramel / enchilada / Harry Potter / church / faint / blood-plates / butterfly needle* and then there's a picture of a smiley face and a series of numbers. I say, "Mother?" and she looks up. I say, "Have you ever seen *A Beautiful Mind*?" and she says, "I don't know. Who's in it?"

I look over at my dad, who's staring at me, the clicking stopped. "That's her, yes. YES. Hahaha," and then *click-click-click*. My mom writes down *A Beautiful Mine* onto the paper and asks if it's about coal or something. I say, "Yes," and walk out the back door to sit in the sun for a bit.

Growing up, my grandparents lived right down the street from me and it seemed that, without fail, any time I drove by, the two of them would be resting on their front porch. When I was a child and full of enough energy to power a small village, I thought this was strange, the idea of people sitting and doing nothing, but today . . . something is going on inside of me. I've been given a gift. Cancer has been a crystal ball into my future and it has said, "Look! Behold! Observe! Here is a glimpse into your life! *THIS* is what it feels like to grow old! Your energies will be sapped and your motivations will run dry! Thank me! Thank me for showing you this!" and in my head I say, "Thank you, Cancer. Thank you for showing this to me. I'll never be the same after this . . . . Thank you."

But today I am the same. Today I have no energy and today I am an old person. I find my sister sitting outside and smoking cigarettes while texting her boyfriend. I sit down next to her but don't say anything. I just push my face into the sky and shut my eyes. The sunlight is as tangible as a warm washcloth.

My sister says, "I love you," and I open my eyes and find her crying. Tears are rolling down her checks like broken faucets and her hands are shaking. I say, "I love you too, Trees—what's—what's wrong? Did you and Jes break up?" and she laughs and makes a noise that sounds like it means, "No." She shakes her head and stares at her feet.

My sister has always been a very emotional person; she's quiet but driven by her heart. She's shy but explosive. There are many things she doesn't care about but the things she *does* invest herself into must be perfect, without flaw, without excuse.

She looks down at her feet and says, "I saw pictures of you that mom had sent over on her phone and you . . . . I'm sorry . . . . You didn't look very good. You looked *sick,* you know," and I say, "Yeah, OK. I mean, I *am* sick," and she says, "You're not *sick! You have CANCER*," and I say, "Had . . . not have."

She looks at me and says, "I showed up and I wasn't expecting my big brother to look like this. In real life you look— I'm sorry . . . so much worse," and I say, "It's my lack of eyebrows that freak you out, huh?" and she laughs a snorty-pig laugh and shakes her head.

"You look really, really terrible and you're my big brother and it's *scaring* me," and then she just breaks down. Meanwhile, my stomach rolls over unexpectedly and I bend over and vomit at my feet, spattering spittle onto my socks.

I say, "Sorry," but my sister just stands up and walks away. Away from the picnic table. Away from me. Away from the backyard, around the house . . . .

. . . And then she's back and I say, "What was that?" and she says, "That was my last cigarette. I'm not—I can't—I'm not smoking anymore, ever again," and I smile, thankful that Cancer is changing the lives of those around me in powerful and positive ways.

CHAPTER 38
TWO FRIENDS, Part 1: ROB

During the summer between my eighth- and ninth-grade years, I ended up meeting a boy my same age named Rob who lived across town from me. He is a mental fixture in my childhood and was a very important part of my adolescence, and although I wrack my brain over and over, I can't seem to recall how the two of us first met. Presently, as a thirty-year-old man, this makes me very sad as I know that things I hold dear to me are beginning to slowly evaporate while I'm not looking.

His parents had divorced long before I knew him, and he was mostly left alone throughout the day during summer break. His mom's small house became our kingdom; its four walls were ours. We could crank the stereo and listen to our music as loud as we wanted. It was that summer that Rob introduced me to Jack Kerouac, Neil Gaiman, and rock and roll.

He would date a girl, I would date a girl, we'd break up with them and date each other's ex-girlfriends; once we even made out with the same girl at the same time, both of us feeling her up while awkwardly trying to avoid each other's hands. That encounter finally ended with the three of us all giving a collective, "This is weird, yeah?" and then driving to Burger King for lunch.

A few years later, Rob and I began to change and grow apart (as people do). He began spending countless hours at the library (pre Internet) researching Buddhism and Hinduism and various forms of monkhood. He claimed to spend hours each day in his room meditating on nothing but clearing his mind and disconnecting from the world.

We'd spend endless hours bickering wildly over the existence and nature of God, me with all of my "hard facts" he was ignorantly overlooking. I would point and condemn, using fear as a weapon. It makes me grimace to remember the things I'd say; the way I'd try to shove a very specific brand of American Christianity down his throat like a horse pill. *"Just take two of these and you'll be fine!"*

Religion was a drug to me. It lifted me up and made me feel good and certain and right. I couldn't get enough – I mean, who doesn't want to feel absolute certainty in the unknown? Certainty gives us a sense of superiority. And superiority damages relationships. And eventually, as most drugs do, it devoured me and alienated my friend. It's funny how religion – a supposedly cosmic belief system based in love, unity and the divine - can separate and isolate human beings so harshly if we allow it to.

Years passed and Rob and I grew further and further apart, only seeing each other randomly in the high-school parking lots. We became involved with different groups of friends but still nodded silently to

330

each other when we passed by happenstance in the halls.

Then, sometime during our junior year, I heard from a mutual friend that he had suddenly taken a bus to California. It wasn't until years and years later that the two of us would meet again, this time at his new home, a Hare Krishna commune in Santa Monica he'd been living in since he left South Dakota. We were different people—both of us half a country away from our hometown, both of us half a decade older, me a bit balder from genetics, he with a purposefully shaved head save for a sprout of hair in the back. I wear a T-shirt and ripped jeans, he an orange robe.

We've both matured as men and are able to discuss our cosmic curiosity's in a more social manner, taking the time to learn from one another rather than attempting merely to teach and talk. He asks me to stay for lunch and we walk through a veritable buffet of vegetarian Indian cuisine and he purchases my meal for me. We say grace together and dig in, reminiscing about people we once knew.

He tells me that he had discovered this temple during one of his various faith studies, contacted them, and they'd sent him an invite along with the bus fare. At seventeen years old he had packed a single bag, got on the Greyhound, and never returned.

Once I was diagnosed with cancer, he and his new wife were one of the very first and very few to come visit us in the hospital. Then, six months later, toward the end of my treatment, he invited my family to his temple for a small lunch. It could not have come at a better time as I was truly feeling as though I needed to unload a minivan of emotional baggage. There were dark things happening deep down in my soul and they were going to come out; Pandora's box was going to crack open. I was feeling very bad things and I needed to say them. I needed to get them into the air around me and I needed someone I trusted to hit them all like Whack-A-Moles when they appeared.

Looking back, I hope to God that these emotions were simply my renegade hormones speaking; my lack of AndroGel and imbalance of testosterone. But even today, years later, I can't say with any absolute clarity. I can't say for certain that I wasn't on the brink of something darker.

Rob, who was now going by the name of Haladhara, and I sat down at a small table while, at my request, our wives and my mother sat down separately. We both say our customary blessing and then I thank him for buying me lunch yet again. He says, "Dude . . . dude . . . c'mon. It's the least I can do."

I look at my large plate with my meager portions and remember the last time I ate here—I had heaping stacks of food. He asks, "How is everything? How are you doing?" and I reach out and pick up a biscuit that might be made out of potatoes and spinach and I take a bite. I say, "I'm not very good, man. I'm not doing very good," and my voice cracks on that last word and he says, "What's wrong?"

I look around the restaurant and see people seated at different tables. My initial fear when we walked in the door had been that I would throw up and make a scene. My new fear is that I was about to start crying uncontrollably with an audience.

I say, "I'm . . . so . . . I don't know. Just inside. Everything feels all weird. It feels all sick," and he says, "But it's gone, yeah? It's all—you're out of it?" and I say, "The cancer is gone . . . but the cancer—it's never been the problem. It's the chemo. The chemotherapy is the monster, and I've got one round left. I don't know if I can do it. I don't know if I have it in me," and Rob, or Haladhara, puts down his food and puts his fingertips together and just listens to me talk. I ramble.

"It hurts so much. I can't walk. I can't talk. I'm . . . pain . . . everything is fuzzy. The ice-cream truck made me cry. Jade is giving me baths. I can't take care of myself. Can't walk. Can barely think, talk . . . . I can't eat. I don't know. If I had to do this again, I can't say, I can't say, I don't know that I wouldn't just . . . kill myself. I don't think I can do it again."

These are the darkest words I've ever spoken and I consider this moment to be my darkest hour. I glance around the small room and find that no one is

333

looking at me but everyone is *paying attention*. I try to stifle my gasps but I have no control over anything. I put my face into my hands and try to hold back visceral wails that seem to be clawing their way out of my very soul. Thinking these monstrous and loathing thoughts is evil and poisonous toxicity— thinking about suicide. Speaking the words out loud feels so much more tangible and dangerous. It feels as though I'm speaking some kind of taboo truth into them that I hate, bringing it to life or somehow birthing it into our world. I don't want to say it, don't want to admit it but I want to get in front of the problem, get it into the air, out in the open; murder it before it murders me.

I am broken.

Rob reaches across the table and puts his hand on mine and says, "You're going to be all right. You're so strong. Everything you're going through is difficult. But you will get through it. You are inspiring."

This moment between two people. This compassion. This empathy. This kindness. This is what God looks like to me.

CHAPTER 38
TWO FRIENDS, Part 2: LUCY

At some point in the early 2000s, my brother-in-law, Jarod, moved to Bozeman, Montana, where he began work as a bartender while attending college. It was at this bar he met a girl and fellow employee named Lucy.

The two hit it off well enough, and when Jarod discovered that she was moving to Los Angeles, he volunteered to connect her with my wife and me.

So one extremely windy day, we all met at a Starbucks and drank overpriced burnt coffee and chatted about our plans to "take over this town." She was one of the nicest people I'd ever met; she wore a constant smile, made well-timed jokes, and laughed when expected. All that aside, we were living in different parts of the city, and the three of us were simply too preoccupied with other things to navigate a new and strange friendship.

It would be years before either Jade or I saw her again.

Fast forward several tax seasons until I'd finally found myself working as the lead editor at a start-up post-production company in Studio City. The owner, an enormously tall Dutchman named Radu, had a weakness for cheeses, *Entourage*, and loose women. He had a constant interest in "The Dakotas," a cowboy land filled with bars, gunfights, and no electricity that I had apparently somehow escaped, presumably on the back of a wild stallion.

He'd wander around the office, ducking through doorways, moving from edit bay to edit bay proclaiming, "Rah-DO-IT!" if he agreed with something you were creating.

A year into my job there, he decided to bring on our very first assistant editor; a young lady named Amber who had just finished college up north and was now trying to get her foot into some steady work.

One Wednesday, Radu called a meeting (which usually just entailed Amber and I sitting at a table in the front lobby while he showed us his favorite moments from *Entourage* and splurged on exotic cheeses) to tell us about a new client we had coming in; some foreign documentary that needed editing. "I know neither of you speaks Spanish—hell, Brookbank barely speaks English—but we're going to just Rah-do-it. You got it?" Honestly, he was like a character out of a TV show.

I reach out for a piece of cheese, and he slaps my hand away. "This ain't no soup kitchen! You pay for that cheese? Were you born in a barn, Dakota? You probably were born in a barn—go buy your own Velveeta cheddar slices, whatever. This is good cheese. Fine, here's one piece, just to try. Savor it because you'll probably not get anymore again. How much you think this cheese platter cost? Forty bucks."

I say, "This cheese tastes like a jock strap," and Radu says, "You have the etiquette of a possum. Shut your mouth when you eat, you rat bastard. Now, listen, the client is Such and Such—" except he actually names the client and doesn't say *such and such* and Amber says, "Such and Such on Miracle Mile?" and Radu says, "Yes; you know them?" and Amber says, "Yeah, my best friend Lucy works there—we graduated from Bozeman together," and I say, "You went to Bozeman? Lucy who?" and Amber says, "Lucy *Such and Such!*" and I say, "Black hair? Thin? Laughs when she's supposed to?" and Amber says, "Yes!" and I say, "My brother-in-law is Jarod. Do you know him?" and she says, "*I know Jarod!*" and Radu says, "I ain't got time for this. I'm going to take a shit. Nobody touch my cheese," and then he leaves the room.

This is how I met Lucy for the second time.

*** *** *** *** ***

There are people that you meet from time to time and you can just tell that karma is out to get them, or is, at the very least, lying dormant and waiting for the perfect time to strike. Then there are people who, conversely, you meet and you just think that even their dandruff should be considered good luck powder in most circles.

Lucy was one of these latter. Although, it should be stated that she does not, so far as I am aware, have dandruff. When you meet her, you immediately think to yourself, "You're a wonderful person. You're happy and you know what happiness is and I can simply tell that you are a good friend with a trustworthy personality."

Over the course of the following years, Lucy and my wife and myself all keep up, fighting through the weirdness that is LA friendships in order to get together for the odd and random dinner. Our friendship matures and Lucy ultimately becomes a close friend of both my wife and myself.

Then, one day, years later, I'm sitting in My Yellow Chair with my blanket when my phone rings and it's Lucy and she's asking if she can come over to visit. *Of course*, we say and when my wife shouts, "*Come in!*" a few hours later, Lucy hobbles into my living room wearing a full blown please-sign-here leg cast.

After the initial, "*What-the-what*?!" and "Is that fer real?!" questions out of the way, she regales us with her tale of woe.

Two nights ago, she says, she was coming home with her roommate. It was about 11 p.m. and she had to park about a block away from her house. "It's a good neighborhood though so not a big deal."

She and her roommate exit the car, begin the track back up the block and—someone punches her in the back of the head, knocking her 110-pound frame to the ground. She rolls over in time to see two young men begin to stomp, literally *stomp* on her leg until it is cracked and broken, only stopping when porch lights begin to turn on from her wretched screaming. The two boys take her purse and disappeared into the darkness while her roommate fumbles with 911.

I say, "They . . . stomped . . . on your leg . . . until it snapped?" and she says, "Yes, with their feet. They just jumped up and down on it. They shattered my leg. And, yes, I'm moving to New York City."

There is silence between us when my wife says, "New York? Isn't that dangerous?" and Lucy says, "I don't know. Probably. Maybe. Certain neighborhoods. I just can't—every day I think they'll be there. Every day, no matter where I am, I'm afraid they'll be there. If I'm in a parking garage at nine p.m. or a Target parking lot at eleven a.m. I think they're following me—I mean, I know they're not following me, but I'm waiting for them to come back. I was mugged and I'm afraid it's going to happen again. I'm afraid of them returning. Do you know what I mean?"

I look at her and I say, "Yes, I know exactly what you mean." I know what it's like to have them return again and again and again. Mine doesn't come in the form of two cowardly men; mine comes in the form of bad news over and over and over. Testicular cancer, surgery, heart cancer, lung cancer, grand mal seizure, fainting, puking, RLS, blood vomiting, insomnia, constipation, atrophy, platelets, blood transfusions, lockjaw.

The process has a way of getting under your skin, into your soul and making you not trust The Good News. Cancer wasn't done with me; it was going to come and find me in some parking lot and finish the job. Lately I'd just been spending my days waiting for the other shoe to drop.

I say, "New York will be awesome. Be safe," and Lucy leaves for her new life where she will find success in producing. I love Lucy's story because it shows that goodness and opportunity can come from anywhere. Two bottom feeders break your leg, steal your purse, and re-route your train for New York where you find more happiness and success than you ever had in Los Angeles. It's a high price to pay, but the even higher price is a life lived in mediocrity.

Feeling suddenly inspired to *make moves* and to *get out there* and to *feel the hustle* that I heard Lucy talking about, I decide to e-mail my boss. I've been in correspondence with him over the last few months, and he, to his great credit, has been nothing short of compassionate. When I had to leave he said, "Go, take as much time as you want. Whatever you need. We'll work with you," and for an employee, that inspires comfort and safety. In an industry where everyone is flaky, it was a breath of fresh air; while dealing with a disease that was unpredictable, it was wonderful to have predictability. It was nice to know that, at the end, my job was there.

I'd hit him up every three to four weeks just to touch base and say hi, let him know I was still alive. He writes back with, "No problem! Just beat that cancer! Quit worrying about the job! It's here! It's yours! Just get better! Good luck!"

So it is upon this day that I write him one final time to give him the good news, "My cancer is gone and it looks like I'm going to wander the Earth for a few more years after all. I should be able to return in about six weeks and I just want to say thank you so much for keeping it open for me."

Our medical bills were now into the hundreds of thousands and we needed a financial Band-Aid *soon*. This job was the only rope I could see that would pull us to safety.

I send the e-mail and I hear the *whoosh* indicating that the digital file is flying through cyber space and I imagine Phil's e-mail giving him a little *bing* notification. I imagine him reading it and smiling and feeling warm and fuzzy that he is such a huge part in helping me to gather the shattered pieces of my life and glue them back together. He can sleep easy tonight knowing that he and he alone was the boat that sailed my job through the storm. He was the captain at sea while I was in the infirmary. I stare at my blank computer monitor and I think, "I hope he knows how much that means to me. I hope I was articulate enough."

BING.

I receive an email. From Phil. *Wonderful*! I quickly open it up, excited for the warm words of encouragement from o captain, my captain. I smile and begin to read, paraphrased as, "Johnny. I'm so glad to hear you're better. Unfortunately, I gave your job away two weeks after you left and didn't have the heart to tell you. I'll put out a couple feelers. Be well. Phil."

I reach over and sip my hot tea, fold my hands and purse my lips as I try to decide what my emotional response should be to this terse letter.

I look toward the door and, nodding, I see our collection of footwear. It appears the other shoe has finally fallen.

CHAPTER 39
FINAL ROUND

At this point I believe that there is nothing that can be said that hasn't already been said before. You, reader, are just as familiar with the routine as I am. Even though this is the last round and the celebratory party hats should, at the very least, be brought out and dusted off, I can't help but feel a strange mourning and lingering.

Even though my mother keeps saying, "This is it, this is it! That's the last time we'll drive through those gates. That's the last time we'll enter these doors. That's the last time you'll check in. That's your last IV. How does it feel?" I can't help but think that this is not The Last. This is just Another. This is just Another Stop that takes me on and on and on. I'm so mentally broken and physically destroyed that the idea of getting off this ride makes no sense to me. I'm so brainwashed by procedure and routine that the idea of the Long Spoken of and Prophesized, Great and Powerful END could not really be here.

Over the last few weeks I've developed a sore throat that stings like rug burn, a side effect I blame fully on the vaporizer. And so, having recently become so conscious of the health of my body, I've decided to give up smoking weed completely in lieu of my own well-being. I don't want any more drugs in my system. I want them all gone and out of me. Everything.

The nausea has been stronger than usual but I fight through it (as though I have a choice), spending days with my eyes closed while focusing on my breathing. Time has lost all relevancy and the clock is just a geographical readout that happens to tell me where the sun is in the sky. I feel every second and am given the chance to stare at it and mull it over, dissect it, assess it, pass it on, examine the next one.

I try to imagine everything that I've missed— the six months of the world that has been existing without me—and I realize in a very sobering way that I do not matter. I am very insignificant in, not only the greater scheme of things, but in the most absolute minutia of life. I am replaceable, interchangeable and forgotten.

No matter what I do or what happens to me, the world will continue to spin, the glaciers will continue to melt, and Coca-Cola will still have bubbles.

I am not invincible.

But I can do anything and there is no longer anything to fear.

CHAPTER 40
THE FINAL DAY

I wake up in a dark room. I am seven years old. I look out the window and there is snow covering the ground. It's fresh. Strange ice patterns have crawled up the glass panels, trying to creep into my home, into my house. I run to the bed next to mine and shake my sister awake. She snorts and sits up, pushing me away. I stand back and say nothing. I just watch her. And then I see the realization dawn on her face. She knows. She's been waiting. And now it's here. It's finally here.

The two of us bound down the stairs together, two at a time, nearly tripping over each other's feet. We each grab the banister and rocket ourselves into the living room where we lay our eyes upon one of the sweetest things an American child will ever see:

A Christmas tree pregnant with gifts.

Oh . . . try to remember, try to remember. The full tree, the red globes. The lights. The stockings. The *presents*. I am seven and this is my currency. These are my diamonds. There are so many boxes of so many shapes and sizes in so many varying brands and designs of wrapping paper. *Where to start*?!

The night before was torture; lying awake in bed, in the dark, staring at the ceiling. *You must sleep!* I tell myself. *Shut your eyes*! But my desperation for what tomorrow brings is too great. I lie in bed until exhaustion overpowers me and, like a robot, my body simply shuts down.

I tentatively reach out and touch the first present, the second present. What's in *the big box*? A Super Nintendo? A go-kart? *A time machine*?! I begin to tear and shred; paper is raining down upon my sister and me as we are swallowed up into a complete endorphin high. Neither of us can hear the other squealing with glee.

All is good. All is happy. Everything is perfect.

This is not a story meant to pluck your heartstrings in a way that says, "Ah, but the seven-year-old did not know what awaited him in twenty years." This story has a bigger purpose than mere parallel emotional trite.

There is a magic in Christmas morning for children. It is something we have all felt and experienced but have lost having grown up. Certainly, Christmas is still fun and warm and inviting as adults but there is something *unique* about the quality in the air as a child that, once gone, can never be recaptured.

But here and now I tell you that, as a twenty-six-year-old man, lying in my bed on the fifth floor of the Arcadia Methodist Hospital on January 15, 2009, I feel like a seven-year-old on Christmas morning. That magic was back.

My time, my journey, my experience, my nightmare was finally coming to an end. The light at the end of the tunnel was not only in sight. It was here. Today. From my initial diagnosis to the final drip-drop of chemotherapy, my grand total was 163 days under the gun—3,912 hours of fire-refining damage control.

I wish I could tell you that there was one single moment where I simply crossed a line or walked out the door and then it was over with a bang, finished like a race. But that's not the case.

This is how Cancer ends.

Not with a bang but a whimper.

A nurse enters, and looking at my final chemo bag, unceremoniously states, "All done."

I shut my eyes and I pull in breath and I sob in happiness for the first time since my brain cancer came back negative. After so much distress and tragedy and bad news piled on top of us, here it is. Tears roll down my cheeks and onto my pillow and my wife squeezes my hand and my mother squeezes my other hand and the three of us have made it through alive.

We. Have. Survived.

The nurse pulls out my IV for the last time, and just like that, I am free. While I'd love to tell you

that it ends there, it doesn't. Because the reality is I'm still very sick. I still have gasoline and particles of nuclear fusion soaring through my veins and it will be weeks before they're out and it will be months before I feel like an actual living human again. Who knows how long it will take for my eyebrows to come back .
. . .

Sue leads my entire nursing staff into the room, six of them total. It is this group of complete strangers that have made me feel as much at home as I possibly could have over the course of the last six months. They've given of their time and energy to help me keep my attitude highest when it wanted to live in the depths of oblivion. They were my cheerleaders, my team, my friends, my family in a time when I needed all of those things. These people went above and beyond their duty to bring me safely to The Other Side. They guided me back across the river Styx.

Sue sets a chocolate cake in front of me and says, "For when you get appetite back." The cake is the most delicious and unappetizing thing I've ever seen and it turns my stomach but I value the personal token of friendship deeply.

I remember the first hospital we'd visited where they'd forgotten my paperwork and I try to imagine what six months under the care of The Careless would have been like. I shudder.

I stand up slowly and individually hug each of them, staining the shoulders of their smocks with my tears. I embrace Sue last, our special mother-nurse and I whisper, "Thank you," in her ear. Her body is small and frail and I realize that I we currently have the same physical build.

She says, "Mike will take you outside. Sit down," and she signals to a wheelchair. The Wheelchair. The Final Wheelchair. Mike steps behind me, grabs the handles and pushes me into the hallway where my wife snaps a photo of me with the group of them. It will become something that I cherish deeply.

Mike begins to push me forward, and Sue says, "See you later," and I turn around and say to her, "Sue, I don't want you to get the wrong idea but . . . I hope I never see you again." She smiles and laughs and says, "Yes . . . . Yes, I hope I never see you again either. Be healthy. Be well!" and then she turns and disappears into another room, with another patient, to change another life.

Mike pushes me to the front door where my mother is waiting for me with the car. I stand up, turn, and shake Mike's hand. He's always been a man of very few words and so he just says, "Good luck," and I say, "Thank you for everything."

I turn and walk out of the hospital and into the light.

PART 5

"Woo-Hoo!"
-Blur

EPILOGUE

The Cancer was gone but—as far as I could tell—nothing had changed. When I got in the car, I still felt sick and we had to pull over twice on the way home for me to throw up. Upon arriving back at the house, I sat in My Yellow Chair and slept wearing my heavy green parka (with a smile on my face).

My wife set the celebratory chocolate cake on the counter with plans to stick it in the freezer, but while I was asleep and while Jade was in the shower and while my mother was outside, my dog pulled it down and ate two-thirds of it.

I never got to taste the cake that I suffered so much for, but my dog looked very happy and slept very well that night.

Slowly, over the course of the next few weeks, my appetite *did* begin to return and I found myself slowly eating more and more, slowly scooping larger and larger portions onto my place, slowly starting to say things like, "In-N-Out for dinner? Steak? Chicken sounds good," although I refused to touch any type of alcohol, and for years afterward, was terrified to put anything in my body that wasn't for purely nutritional value. In fact, I became so entirely hyperconscious of the state and condition of my food that I insisted we get rid of the microwave.

My wife approaches me one night and says that a friend of ours from high school who was now living in Oregon had given us an open invitation to visit her. We jointly decided that this was an ideal point to begin our If Not Now, When? Adventures.

My mother agreed to stay at our home for an additional week to watch our dogs and we hit the road. It was a beautiful and memorable journey up the coast. I look back at photos from that particular road trip and it amazes me to see that it *literally* looks like my wife was traveling with another man; someone who smiled and laughed but was emaciated and pale. While I was eating better, the weight simply wasn't pouring back on. Even after gaining ten pounds I was still six feet tall and weighing in at a buck forty.

On our journey we began to talk about baby names and, when we got back, it was that conversation that finally led to us take the paternal plunge. After speaking with the fertility clinic, they informed us that we had eleven completely fertilized eggs that were frozen and ready to implant. I stare at the phone as a single phrase that I'd heard from a woman at church months and months ago echoes through my mind. "I see babies. Lots and lots of babies."

In February 2010 we began the initial stages of in vitro fertilization and three months later we found out we were pregnant.

With twins.

The pregnancy and delivery were both textbook. Jade went full term and on January 6, 2011, Quinn Marie was born two minutes before her brother, Rory James.

Becoming a father and raising twins has been an adventure in its own right that could (and maybe will?) fill a book. My children are wild and savage and inquisitive beings. Their personalities could not be further apart and every day with them is living life in a full, bright spectrum of color.

Every single day with them has been completely insane in the best way possible, and I have Cancer to thank. Without Cancer I never would have banked. Without Cancer we never would have done IVF. Without Cancer we never would have implanted two eggs.

And now, knowing the life I have, knowing what Cancer brought me, I would roll through it all again if it meant being given the opportunity to raise the two of them together.

Just after the Twinkies turned two, we decided to revisit the fertility clinic and walk through the process again. This time, out of fear that we would become the parents of *two* sets of twins we only implanted a single egg, which stuck temporarily before we suffered a miscarriage several weeks later.

Tragedies cannot be compared and I can't tell you that a miscarriage is worse than cancer is worse than my grandfather passing. They are not better or worse, they are simply different perspectives of loss. Each tragedy a unique experience that calls out to us and seems to embed itself in the very threads of our DNA, forcing us to carry it around for the rest of our time on the planet.

A few months later we tried a second time for a third child, again with only a single egg. The results came back positive and for the next nine months we held our baited breaths nervously until October 7, 2013, when Bryce Alison entered the universe.

Every day I have on this Earth, with my wife, with my children, with my family, with myself, is an absolute gift and it's something that I'll never take for granted. Everything is beautiful and every day is an adventure. I have had the rare gift to glimpse death in the face, see what my life is worth to me, and then stand up from the table and walk away.

Thoughts of cancer follow me everywhere and the reminders are constant; every time I hear The Ice-Cream truck drive down the street, every time I see the reality show about the family with all the kids, every time I drive past the Wiltern in LA where we saw Ben Folds Five, every time I hear the music of Ben Folds Five, every time someone says the word *Arcadia*, every time someone mentions Las Vegas or Kings of Leon or the words *saline solution* or ninjas or George Harrison or the word *flood*. These things and many, many more are all instant triggers and not a day goes by that something doesn't drop a red flag and send me back to It. And I'd have it no other way. My baggage is a constant reminder that every day is not a good day to die. But that doesn't mean that it *isn't* my day to die. Because it just might be. Death opens its arms wide and simply pulls in what it can, like an enormous whale consuming krill.

Every day I hug my children. Every day I say "Yes" to opportunity. Every day I embrace the unknown. Everyday I contemplate and cast wonder at the magnificent and magical world around me, the good and the evil, all wrapped up together, living in all things around us, breathing, eating and existing in beautiful and marvelous complexity.

I look at my life—I look at what has come before cancer and I see all the things I wanted to do. When I was in high school I had hoped to someday buy a van and just head out, to drive without direction or purpose. I wanted to write things and create things and live a life that pushed my boundaries of experience and culture and . . . then I got a job that locked up my time and helped to strangle my ambitions.

I was diagnosed with stage 4 cancer. I was looking down the barrel of a gun and pleading for my life and swearing that, yes, when I came through the other end, things would be different and I wouldn't be so complacent about my life and I wouldn't be bored or boring and I would do all the things that needed to be done and say the things that needed to be said and if I died with a list of regrets when I was ninety or eighty or seventy or thirty-five, that list would be incredibly short and pathetic and would contain only random and asinine things like "Eat a pizza from the inside out" because I planned to live the rest of my days chasing daily adventure.

I told myself that I would start a family. And I have. I told myself I would pursue directing. And I have. I've directed short films and music videos and have worked with musicians whose work inspires me and have gotten my work into film festivals and my music videos featured on *Rolling Stone*. I've started a production company and created commercial spots that air nationally on broadcast television. I chased that dream and I caught it. I told myself I would read *Moby Dick*. And I have. And it was the worst thing ever but I finished it and can say with utter confidence that you should never pick it up. I told myself I would read *Grapes of Wrath*. And I have. And it's one of the best things ever and I can say with utter confidence that you *should* pick it up. I told myself that I would tell my father that I loved him more often, and even though for some reason it's very difficult for sons and fathers to say these things to one another, I have. I told myself I would start camping. And I have. I've taken my family on meandering, aimless, vacations in a minivan and I can finally high five that teenage version of myself.

I've written television pilots and recorded podcasts and learned to cook and had '80s-themed parties and made new friends that have become my family and have started a blog and am learning to play the guitar and the ukulele and I play hide and seek at least once a week. I've started playing Frisbee golf and hiking and I just got a membership to a gun range where I have learned that I prefer a revolver to a pistol but my accuracy is superior with a rifle. I recently killed and cleaned my first fish and by the light of three headlamps, I gutted and cooked it with my bare hands before feeding it to my tribe. I flew to Nicaragua, slept at the base of a volcano, went zip lining, and helped a woman who was being mugged.

I read. Every day. Sometimes out loud with my wife. I write. Almost every day. I keep a journal but I almost never read it. I go to concerts and the theater and I say yes to any strange food that happens across my plate, which is how I ended up eating blood sausage and frog meat. I started a financial budget with my wife and we've done a pretty decent job of sticking to it. I love those around me every day because I almost lost each and every one of them.

My mantra has become *Year of the Yes.* Whenever someone asks me to do something that I've never done the answer is yes, yes, yes, always yes. I want to live strong and loud and uncomfortable. I want to find my boundaries and push past them and expand my culture and thoughts and experiences and love for all of humanity and the energy of life itself.

I never want to say that I am *too old* or *too tired* or *too busy* to go attempt something or to succeed at something or to fail at something. Too old and too tired and too busy are excuses invented by lazy people with no personal ambition. Age is relative. Time is relative. Even success is relative. But what we do with our time is not. Every move counts.

Life is too short to be stagnant and The End already comes too swiftly. When Death finally knocks on my front door, beckoning me home, I want to smile broadly, look at my to-do list and I want the last words I see to be, "Embrace Death. You did everything."

SPECIAL THANKS

Scott Chrisman
Donna Fischer
June Greenwood
Brittany McConnell
Tiffany Morgan
Heidi Ryder
Moira Paris
Chandra Wicke
Barbara Cunningham

Made in the USA
San Bernardino, CA
29 October 2018